Time to Fly!

About the Author

Neil O'Brien left school and took the first job he was offered which was in a bank. He worked there for 23 years and then decided that it was time for a change. In 1998 he left the safe and secure bank job and founded his company called Time to Fly. He is now an international speaker and coach in the areas of change and transformation, resilience and confidence, self-belief and self-worth. For more information, see www.timetofly.ie.

TIME TO FLY!

7 Exhilirating Lessons to Take Your Life to the Next Level

Neil O'Brien

The Liffey Press

Published by
The Liffey Press Ltd
Raheny Shopping Centre, Second Floor
Raheny, Dublin 5, Ireland
www.theliffeypress.com

© 2012 Neil O'Brien

A catalogue record of this book is
available from the British Library.

ISBN 978-1-908308-33-7

Printed in the UK by TJ International.

Contents

Foreword

It feels appropriate that I write this foreword on a plane flying at 39,000 feet that's taking me from Sydney back home to London.

Neil O'Brien is a friend of mine. He's the sort of friend you feel fortunate to have. He's always there for you. He sees who you are. He genuinely cares about you. He wants you to fly.

I've known Neil for about twelve years. We share a lot of the same interests. We both love inquiry. We are interested in the big conversations about purpose, happiness, love and success. We both support West Ham Football Club. You have to be a philosopher when you support our team. We both love golf. Neil plays golf like he lives his life: he hits long and straight, has a light touch around the green, is inventive when he needs to be, and is solid with the putter.

I'm so pleased Neil wrote this book. *Time to Fly* has been a long time coming. I've had to be patient. Years ago the conversation was, "You could write a great book, Neil." And then it was, "I think you should write a book, Neil." After that it was, "When are you going to start?" And then, "I'm so pleased you've started." And, eventually, "When's the book coming out?" The timing is always perfect. And I trust that you are reading this book at precisely the right time in your life.

Neil has written a great book. He uses the metaphor of flying to show us how we can raise our thinking and live at a higher altitude. Neil's writing style is part biographical and part workbook. He wants you to think about the story of your life and also to take practical action. Neil discovered a potential for greatness in him, and realised that this greatness lives in each one of us, including you. Naturally, when you learn to fly it becomes your joy to help others do so too.

Neil's message is that it's your time to fly. That must be true, or else you wouldn't have this book in your hand. Remember, the timing is always perfect. Neil is ready to join you at the rocky edge. *Time to Fly* is your sacred parchment, full of timeless wisdom and practical help, for this next stage in your journey. What Neil shares with you is not just pleasant theory; it's born from his practical experience. Neil helps people to fly every day in his life. And now he can help you too because he has written this great book.

Thank you Neil.

Robert Holden
author of *Happiness NOW*,
Shift Happens! and *Authentic Success*.
London, August, 2012

Acknowledgments

My business Time To Fly Ltd and also this book would not have been possible without the help and support of many wonderful people:

My parents, Vera and Bert O'Brien, and my brother Carl, for their unwavering support and encouragement.

Michael Conlon and Maria O'Sullivan for giving me the room to develop. Ian Kingston for giving me the kick in the arse. Conor O'Connell and Libby Finlay for helping me to the next level.

Conor Morris and Mervyn O'Shaughnessy of The Sales Institute of Ireland for their continued support and trust.

The Institute of Bankers in Ireland for supporting me from day one.

Robert Holden, Ben Renshaw and Nick Williams for seeing something in me that I couldn't see.

Ian Lawlor and Keelan Cunningham for their openness and generosity. David Storrs for his support and professionalism.

Stephen 'Ski' Wade, the best sport psychologist I know. Niall Kearney and Sheena McIlroy, the best golfers I know. Mary McKenna MBE for just being Mary.

Four 'SuperDubs', Pillar Caffrey, Dessie Farrell, John O'Leary and Tommy Carr, for inviting me inside the ropes. Kelly Proper for her inspiration and honesty.

The O'Malleys and Corkerys for turning up at everything I do. Lucy Foley who's always there too. To Stephen McConnell, the best Bank Manager in the world!

Warren Fox for his energy and optimism. Debbie Deegan for her electrifying presence. Paul Raleigh for his faith and Marilyn Phillips for her certainty.

Frances Keane for her enthusiasm and awesome business acumen. The Pi Group, Andrew Keogh, Don Harris, Mark Donovan, Deiric McCann and Cathy Winston, for being behind me for every page of this book. David Givens of The Liffey Press for taking a punt on a rookie like me.

To Declan McCulloch and Don Harris, my bestest, longest and very oldest friends, for their caring, concern, support and patience.

Finally, to Francesca and Lorenzo. Francesca's wonderful creativity combined with her awesome work ethic constantly pushes me forward. Lorenzo's razor sharp sense of humour and his thoughtfulness for other people is a great example for me to follow. Thanks guys, Love Dad.

I dedicate this book to Angela. As in all parts of my life she is there to give whatever is needed. Thank you my Strong Angel.

Goodbye Comfort, Hello Panic!

Let's start with the big one! The number one thing that prevents human beings from doing anything differently, changing their ways or achieving more of something. This block is so successful and works so well that it has appeared in every coaching relationship I've been involved with. Regardless of whether the relationship was business, sport or life coaching, whether it was an individual or a team, this block arises at some point in the work.

The Comfort Zone

It is of course the Comfort Zone, and I'd like to share with you my interpretation and in particular my experience of this model.

A comfort zone is an area of safety and comfort, and as long as we stay there we feel safe. Of course, we are very busy in this zone – it's not like we are doing nothing and just being a couch potato all the time, far from it. So, while it is an area of safety it is also a rating – a safety rating if you wish. It is a rating of how good we think we are at coping within all the roles we have to play and all the situations in which we find ourselves.

We all have many roles we have to perform. Some of my roles are husband, father, son, brother, god-father, presenter, writer, sales person, coach, friend and so on. And, the situations we find our-selves in are a mix of planned and spontaneous events. So as you can see we have many comfort zones and they are all different sizes depending on our perceived level of competency and capa-bility. In other words, there are some things in life I am terrible at and struggle to cope with so my comfort zone would almost be just a dot on a page, and there are some things I am world-class at, these comfort zones would be the size of a building! So where do they come from and how can they be different sizes?

If you think of it as an equation then the comfort zone (or 'rating') is what you get when you add past experience (p ex) to self-worth (sw). See figure 1 below.

$$p\ ex + sw = cz$$

Fig 1

If you are in a role (or a situation) that you don't think you're good enough for, you are basing this on your perception of some past experience, and if you are also experiencing low self-worth, then your area of competency (comfort zone) will be quite small and limiting. As a result, you won't have much self-confidence or self-belief because you are already telling yourself that you are no good at this!

By the way, if I am coaching you and challenging you to change, I have no room to manoeuvre with your past experience; you'll de-fend your past experience to the death! But that's OK because I have all the room to manoeuvre I need in the area of self-worth. If you don't know how self-worth works then it can change on the hour and also at the whim of others. We will look at self-worth in detail later on so just keep it in mind for now.

Risk-Free Zone

Note also that there are no risks within the comfort zone; it is an area of safety and predictability. As there are no risks then you don't need any confidence to operate at this level, so this means that the opportunity to create confidence is not available within an area of comfort and safety. As I said earlier, it's still a busy and challenging place to be but ultimately it is all 'auto-pilot' stuff – easy-peasy-lemon-squeezy!

The Panic Zone

Now all of the above is by way of introduction because the comfort zone becomes really interesting when you find yourself outside it. You are now in another zone and there's always more of this zone than there is of comfort – Welcome to the Panic Zone! Or, as Star Wars fans would say: Welcome to the Dark Side! See figure 2.

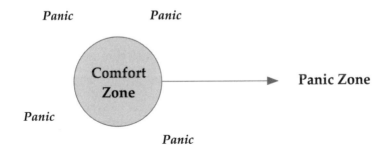

Fig 2

If the comfort zone is safe, comfortable and cosy, the panic zone is uncomfortable and full of panic, tension, stress and anxiety! I recently heard the following lovely definition of anxiety which works really well here:

'Anxiety is excitement without the breathing.'

That sums up really well what the panic zone feels like.

When I workshop this topic and ask the attendees for examples of what could happen tomorrow that would force them into the panic zone the following are the typical responses – at home it would be a crisis, an illness, an unexpected visitor staying for a month. Work examples included being asked to speak at an event, a difficult customer, a complaint, a difficult conversation, a new role, new job or a new location. I'm sure we could develop this list further but you get the drift.

Three Ways Out

But, it is important to note that there are three categories of ways that you end up in the panic zone. All of the above examples are only of one category. The three categories are: Scared Out of Comfort, Excited Out of Comfort and Panic Because It's Going Too Well.

Scared Out of Comfort

The above examples are of the 'scared out' variety. That is, they are things 'done to us'. They weren't our idea, and through no fault of our own we've still been put in an uncomfortable position. This is the panic zone.

In fact, during a recent workshop one participant said after I mentioned the public speaking example and created a pretend scenario that her CEO asked her to speak at an event to 5,000 people in a month's time that she would resign from her job and become unemployed rather than have to face this challenge – a big leap from comfort into panic!

Excited Out of Comfort

So as you can see the 'scared out' examples are easy to think of and are the ones that people mention first, but there is this category too. 'Excited out' is where we decide to take action, we initiate something, we are masters of our own destiny and we make the first move even when knowing that it will lead to discomfort and stress. However, because we are driving this change it also feels exciting and adventurous. Some examples are:

Job or career change, standing up for yourself, setting exciting goals or plans for the future, starting something new, going somewhere different, changing or improving a habit or, are you ready for this, speaking to 5,000 people in a month's time!

Goodbye Bank, Hello World

In my case, the 'excited out' option happened when I left my permanent, pensionable successful bank job after 23 years. At age 40 I decided that it was time for a change. I was really well prepared for this change but I still panicked when it happened. In fact, I panicked for about nine months. The reason for this panic I will come to later but it had its foundation in low self-worth and low self-confidence. So even the 'excited out' option can still be scary, it's just that it's a more exciting variety of panic.

'It's Going Too Well'

This is the category that takes 'excited out' to a whole new level. This is when things start excitingly well and then just kept going. This is when we are waiting for the 'bubble to burst' or 'there'll be tears before bedtime'. I have worked with sports people who panicked because they started really well, sales people who panicked because they're having a great year and a woman who panicked because her new boyfriend loved her too much! So this category is about how much success, happiness, love and so on can you take before you start to question it? Before you wonder if you deserve it?

What about Confidence?

There is an extra element to this 'leaving the comfort zone business'. Let's start with the 'scared out' option first. As I've stated above we get scared out of comfort into panic but it's not all bad news. If we cope well with the panic then we are gaining the experience of surviving and succeeding in tough times. As we gain experience we are then also learning something. OK, these are tough lessons and this form of learning never feels like 'learning' at the time, but there is still some value to be gained from it. However, there is one thing missing and that is that this route does not increase confidence.

On entering the global economic recession of 2008 and beyond Ireland was scared out of comfort into panic. The country is now finally coming to terms with this and learning to succeed in the panic zone, but Ireland is not becoming more confident.

The only route to more confidence is by instigating the move at the outset; in other words, by being excited and motivated out of comfort, by being masters of our own destiny and retaining some level of ownership and responsibility from the start.

Say YES to Panic to Say YES to Confidence

So if you want to really fast-track your development of self-confidence and self-belief then it is really important that you decide to make a change. There will be enough times for us to be scared out, they are probably queuing up already, but the issue is: how often do we choose confidence, panic and success?

Two Choices – Choose Wisely

Most times we find ourselves in the panic zone we have two choices: 1. Stay in the panic zone and learn to cope and then succeed, or 2. Return to comfort. Workshop participants have also described these choices as fight or flight, or sink or swim. These work well too. However all of this is just by way of introduction to the comfort zone model. The real action starts now because there is something else about the comfort zone that you need to know now.

Expand or Shrink – You Choose

The boundary of the comfort zone is always moving but it moves so slowly that human beings are not good at realising that it is moving until later. In other words, our comfort zones are either expanding or shrinking, depending on what direction we are travelling in. Let me remind you that the comfort zone is an area of comfort, safety and cosiness, but it can also become a trap.

Expand and Grow

You and I don't grow or develop anything in the comfort zone because, as I mentioned earlier, there are no risks in this zone so no confidence is required. And when there are no risks there is a loss of confidence, therefore there is an avoidance of adventure. No new behaviours are required which results in no growth or expansion taking place. In other words, you've got to be prepared to get outside the comfort zone first for growth to follow. See figure 3.

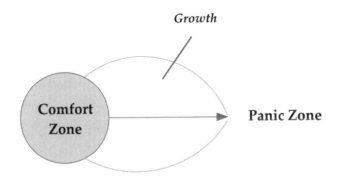

Growth

Comfort Zone

Panic Zone

Fig 3

An example here might be useful. Imagine you run your own business. There will be times when you'll have to make changes to how your business operates or how you sell your goods and services to continue to grow, develop and challenge the competition. This may involve taking some calculated risks and may involve having to do 'uncomfortable things'. Just because they are uncomfortable doesn't make them wrong, but what is guaranteed is that you'll learn from these actions even if they don't go particularly well. If there's learning taking place then, as we've seen above, confidence and growth are happening also.

It's just that it doesn't feel like it at the time!

Shrink and Reduce

This is the other choice, which is essentially staying put within your comfort zone. Now I should mention right here that there are times in life when you and I should stay deep within our comfort zone and allow ourselves to be taken care of. If we suffer a trauma or a tragic loss then we must allow healing to take place and this healing will take as long as it needs. So in this case we should stay safe and comfortable. But, in most other situations we need to question our need for comfort.

In fact, if you want more or less of anything you must be prepared to get a little uncomfortable to achieve it.

However, back to shrink and reduce. Let's use an example: You've decided that there is a colleague who takes complete advantage of you – your good humour, your good nature, your willingness to help, your availability. And you've decided you are going to have a serious word with him in work the next day at 3.00 pm 'when things quieten down a little'. You are determined to lay down some new rules and boundaries, and while you're at it you're going to get a lot off your chest! You phone me to tell me this the day before and we agree that you will phone me afterwards to let me know how it went.

Cosmic Test

But, during our phone call there was another entity, another parallel universe, listening in. This universe is called 'life', and life's job is to test commitment. So, at some point between our phone chat and the planned conversation there's going to be a cosmic test to see if you are serious about this, to see if you are courageous enough and want it badly enough. In fact, to see if you really can make a stand for yourself.

Anyway, you get up that morning and remind yourself that if you achieve nothing else today at least you're going to 'have the talk' at 3.00 pm. So you get out to work and you do everything you'd normally do and then just when you're making yourself a quiet cuppa before you launch into the day, what happens? The colleague in question arrives, simply by chance (but is it really?) to make a cuppa too! What's more, there is nobody else around – there must be a practise fire drill on somewhere that both of you are not required for! So, life is now saying, 'this is not going to happen neat and tidy in an office at 3:00 pm when it suits you best and you are well prepared, no, let's do it right now!' And just to make matters even more difficult, the other person is being really nice. In fact, they've never been this nice before! Welcome to the cosmic test.

In this situation what do most of us do most of the time? Yep, you've guessed it, we wimp out! In that moment we convince ourselves that 3:00 pm will be better – we'll be better prepared, it'll be better in an office than at the coffee machine, it's important to be professional about these things, mustn't cause a scene, and so on. In fact, we may even start to think that because they were nice maybe they've changed, maybe they've had a vision, reached enlightenment on the way to work, maybe it's been you all the time, maybe . . . we don't need to have 'the talk' at all?

3:00 pm

Of course 3:00 pm arrives, the queue is out the door, the phone is ringing off the hook, you need to go to the toilet, the office isn't free and 'he' looks in bad form. In that moment you decide that now isn't a good time and you promise yourself that Tuesday fortnight would be much better.

Shrink-Wrap

What has just now happened is that you have shrunk within that relationship. The other person of course is completely unaware of all of this but you now have that 'hollow feeling' in your chest. The feeling that tells you that yet again you haven't stood up for yourself. In fact, within that relationship you will also find other things difficult to do that were once within your confidence range are now other things you'll avoid. So your comfort zone is now shrinking in around you leaving you less and less space to perform, to be authentic, to be assertive.

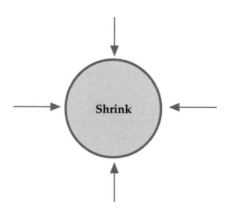

Fig 4

Retreat to Safety

In returning to our above example, it later turns out that the colleague did not reach enlightenment or even mature a little, no, 'the talk' still needed to happen. But, the longer you wait for the 'right time', the right day, the right planetary alignment, the talk seems to be getting more difficult to do. In reality it isn't; the same things need to be said. No, what's really happening is that you are retreating from it, backing away from it. It's getting further away and therefore more challenging. But of course, you know that when you do have the talk it very often is not as bad as you think it's going to be. So it didn't change but you did. You retreated to comfort and safety waiting for the 'right time'.

Difficult Conversations

I recently finished a series of one-day workshops for all of a bank's branch managers and assistant managers, about 20 workshops with 10 attending each one. The purpose of these workshops was to help the attendees with their 'Mental Fitness in Difficult Times'. They were great to run with full engagement from all and proved to be a huge success. There was one element of these workshops however that's worth mentioning. Essentially, each workshop finished with 'homework' to be completed during the following month and then they had to report to me their experiences.

The 'homework' was to be a mix of work- and life-based actions but in either case the theme was that they were to 'do things they've been avoiding or putting off'. A theme quickly emerged in that the most common thing that people had been avoiding in work and life was – difficult conversations. And the work ones weren't difficult conversations with customers. No, it was difficult conversations with colleagues that was the issue. And the situation at home was similar.

I'm delighted to report that, as a result of the workshop, over 400 difficult conversations (work and home) took place that may otherwise not have happened!

So, if the above example rings true for you, you are not alone. It seems that difficult conversations are uncomfortable for many of us a lot of the time. Why is this?

(Well I have an explanation and it will follow in a later chapter on low self-worth, including the need to be popular rather than respected, trying too hard to please people and so on.)

Too Busy!

Having outlined all of the above it's probably only fair that I give you both sides of this principle, so the following is the best and most regular cop-out I've met over the years in this area. If you ever want to avoid panic and discomfort get *really busy*. If anyone ever enquires if you've had 'the talk' or done the thing you said you'd do, just tell them that you've been *too busy* and they'll let you away with that because the chances are they've been really busy too!

You see, this is how we live with ourselves and also how we temporarily lose that hollow feeling of self-defeat that I mentioned earlier. We justify to ourselves our inability to take that action by completing many other actions. Of course, none of them are as important, but if you add up loads of tiny 'importances' then maybe they add up to a replacement? By the way, have you noticed that if you are waiting for something – a bus, a train, a plane, a doctor – getting really busy helps the time to pass quickly? So staying in our comfort zone is a really clever way to 'kill time' while waiting or avoiding something.

In Summary –

✪ The **Comfort Zone** is a rating of our competency in certain situations. Its size is determined by the addition of past experience to self-worth. The comfort zone is when we operate and perform at a level and pace that's comfortable for us. There are no risks in the comfort zone, therefore there is no extra confidence created either.

✪ The **Panic Zone** is outside the comfort zone. There is always more panic zone than comfort zone. The panic zone is made up of panic, tension, stress and anxiety.

✪ You can be **excited out** of comfort or, you can be **scared out**. You can then choose – stay, cope and then succeed despite the discomfort, or return to comfort, the way things used to be.

✪ To grow and develop anything you will have to get uncomfortable first, that is, take action. Leave your comfort zone and it will eventually follow and expand. This is the excited out and growth option. **Growth only happens from discomfort**.

✪ Stay in your comfort zone, moan about your bad luck, talk about taking action but never doing it – this is the **shrink option**. You are now leaking confidence, assertiveness and a sense of adventure. Do this long enough in a relationship or in a job and your comfort zone will shrink in around you until you are wrapped so tight it feels like shrink-wrap.

✪ The **Cosmic Test** is always there to test your commitment, your determination and your courage. Remember, it's only a road test not a road block.

✪ **Difficult conversations** are very often the most uncomfortable things we have to face. They seem to get tougher the longer we wait, but this is only an illusion. It hasn't changed but you have retreated making it seem further away and more elusive.

✪ Don't fool yourself by being **busy waiting** or **busy avoiding**.

✪ Again, if you want to grow and develop you've got to be prepared to **get uncomfortable** first. I'll meet you in the panic zone!

<u>The Law of the Comfort Zone</u>

The objective of life is growth, not comfort; this is the objective of business too.

Warning: The longer you wait, the more uncomfortable it becomes.

Flying Lesson # 2

A Word in Your Eye!

As you've seen, the Comfort Zone is the main block to human beings taking action or changing their ways. There is another block that works in tandem with the comfort zone theory and that is Perception.

Perception

Simply put, perception is the meaning you give to such things as people's behaviour or events that take place. It is your interpretation of these things that becomes your perception, so perception is completely subjective. More on this later, but for now it's worth noting that perception is the greatest block to the potential of anything. It can also exist sometimes at the edge of the comfort zone, hence its link to the first Flying Lesson. So in this Flying Lesson we will look at what perception is, how it works, how it holds us back and what to do about it. To get us started, and to illustrate the laws of perception at work, we are going to do two exercises. The first one is an actual coaching assignment I was involved with, and the second one is some fun with a diagram.

'I Can't Score Here'

At one time I was working with a top Gaelic football team as their mental coach during their championship campaign. I was in the dressing room with the team with just minutes to go before a particular match when one of our top players came up to me and asked, 'have you got a minute?' I said, 'of course' and brought him to a quiet corner of the dressing-room. When I looked at him I noticed that he was white as a sheet and had a look of terror in his eyes. After he checked that no one was within hearing range he leaned over to me and whispered, 'I can't score here.'

He was one of our top players and we would expect him to score something in every game, if not a goal or two definitely some points. For him to say that he can't score was a problem for the team.

So exercise number 1 is: Let's pretend you were in my position. You are the mental coach for this team. What would you say to him next? Remember, the match is starting in 20 minutes, it's the most important game of the year, and the team needs him to play well and score. Let me also remind you that he's panicking and that this is not the time for the 'why' question. He needs a strategy from you right now, in this moment. What would you say to him?

When I 'workshop' this example with a room of participants the following are their suggestions for him:

"Ask him what pitch he loves to play at and tell him to pretend he is there.'

'Remind him that it is a team effort and not to think it all rests on him.'

'Tell him that we believe in him.'

'Tell him that he wouldn't be on this team if he wasn't good enough for this.'

Another participant recently told me that she would 'slap him', and the woman beside her said that she would 'slap him and then give him rescue remedy!' (A herbal relaxation remedy).

So let me continue with what actually happened next. I knew that we still had a final, very short warm-up on the pitch left before the match so my suggestion was:

'Get your hands on every football we've brought and score as many times as you can before the match starts.'

I quickly explained that I hoped that his 'muscle memory' skills could override his mental memory skills, and that we could fool his body into thinking that he loves to score here. I included one condition:

'You must score with every attempt. Don't attempt from 40 yards out, get right in front of the posts (where you can't miss) and score into an open goal from there. You're body doesn't know that it doesn't count but it may inadvertently "record" a miss.'

Out we went on to the pitch to a fantastic reception from the 82,000 people in attendance (the capacity of the Croke Park stadium in Dublin and it's only an amateur sport by the way!) and he did exactly what I asked him to do: he scored 12 times in practice.

Twenty minutes later the match starts. I recorded in my notebook that day that he had seven genuine, solid attempts to score during the game and scored two points (missing five). When the match was over (we had won) he came over to me with his kit-bag over his shoulder and said:

'See, told ya, I can't score here.'

The two points he had scored his brain did not compute and he wanted to spend the evening boring us all about the five he missed. This may seem odd but this is how perception works, and in your own way you are the same as him. All will be explained soon but for now let's do the other exercise.

Have a look at figure 5 and decide what the diagram represents. What is it about? What does it mean? No rush, take your time.

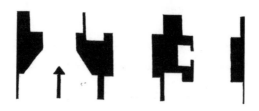

Fig 5

What if we rotate it (figure 6)? Does that help? When you see it differently does it change its meaning?

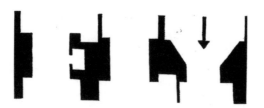

Fig 6

Again, during workshops, participants have suggested the following:

'Is it a motorway? Is the arrow where you come off the motorway?'

'Is it the terminal buildings at Heathrow?'

'Do all the bits fit together to form a logo?'

'Is it a jigsaw?'

'Is it a key and lock mechanism?'
(A group of engineers suggested this).

'Office furniture?'

'Buildings enlarged from an ordinance survey document?'

And school kids have told me the following, starting at the right-hand side and working back to the left:

'A bullfighter's hat, then a crab on the beach, then a wood-burning stove and finally Pocahontas! She's a Native American Indian and she would have an arrow!'

All of these are fantastic and make sense to some degree but they are also missing the point and not the answer I'm looking for. The answer is that the diagram only contains a word, a three-letter word, and the word is ... FLY.

The black in the diagram is only the space between the letters which are in white. Don't feel foolish or stupid if you struggled with this exercise, and don't feel too superior if you got it in one! I will explain what happens when you look at this diagram, why it happens and the implications for footballers, for you and for me. For those of you who are still unsure I offer you figure 7 to help:

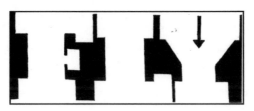

Fig 7 (FLY ruled off)

Now that you've done the two exercises (footballer, FLY), I will link them together when I explain how perception works because they are both exercises in perception.

'Seeing is Believing' – and That's the Problem

Firstly, it's worth noting from the FLY exercise that just because you can't see something doesn't mean it's not there. Just because you couldn't see the word FLY doesn't mean it's not there; what was happening was that your brain gets busy looking for something else. There was a moment there when you would have refused to believe there was a word on the page. You've been 'trained' all your life into the mindset of 'seeing is believing', and if you can't 'see' something you'll tend to deny its existence. You also know the fixed position implied by 'I'll believe it when I see it', but the diagram has just proven how limiting, misleading and inaccurate this position can be.

Could this be happening in work and life for you right now? Are you busy looking for something else and missing something that's right in front of your face?

Seeing the Invisible

Just because you struggle to see your uniqueness and your potential doesn't mean it's not there. Just because you can't see how you can become an amazing success at something doesn't mean that the answer isn't there. Perhaps your brain is on another track right now, but what if you became able to get on track, see things differently and see yourself differently? What if you could develop the ability to see the invisible, to see something (that has always been there) for the first time? This Flying Lesson is about how to see the invisible, but first I must explain how your brain works!

You'll See What Your Mind is Looking for

Now 'the brain stuff': When you looked at the FLY diagram for the first time, even though it was upside-down, your eyes instantly saw the word FLY – we know this because you can now easily see FLY upside-down. Your eyes saw the word FLY and transmitted that information at 250 kilometres per hour to your brain. But perception is determined by your brain, not your eyes. In other words, it's your brain that decides what your eyes see and then filters out everything else, especially if it thinks it's not important to you today. So in fact we can say that you'll see what your mind is looking for. If your mind was looking to make sense of the 'black information', thinking it's the most important, then it completely ignored the 'white information' (the word FLY). The white information blurred off the page, and if you can't see it you believe it doesn't exist!

I'm afraid it gets even worse than this because once you decide that there's no word there you start to set up a 'mindset' to this effect which results in your 'need to be right'. Let me illustrate what I mean with the following diagram.

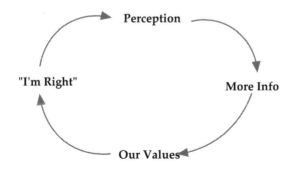

Fig 8

The Perception Flow

✦ Form a perception (250 kph) of a person or event, then

✦ Collect more information, then

✦ Compare what you've just found out to your own set of beliefs and values, then defend

✦ Your need to be right.

Collecting information is very logical and quite objective, comparing to values and beliefs is logical and becoming subjective and the need to be right is very emotional and very subjective. So it's not where we started that's the point, it's where we finish – that's both the issue and the challenge.

Remember the footballer example earlier? His need to be right was stronger than his desire to succeed, which is very emotional and not at all logical. His own belief system and his reluctance to 'rise above' the situation to 'see' it differently were holding him back more than anything else; hence his self-perception was blocking his own potential, which I mentioned at the very start of this lesson.

It's Written All Over You!

When the time came for me to leave the bank where I had worked for 23 years and follow my dream, I had to go through the resignation process. I did my resignation letter at home on a Sunday evening and gave a brilliant 30 minute speech to the cat in the kitchen. The next day I got into work early, phoned my boss and asked if I could see him as soon as possible, that 'there was something I needed to discuss with him'. He said 'now is good and could I drop up immediately'. I had worked directly for this person for nine years (known him for 20) and he had no idea what was coming, but he knew by looking at me that something was up.

He invited me to sit down but I declined – I couldn't until I delivered my speech. I was really nervous; I'm about to resign from the only job I've ever had! I was also worried that he might try to talk me out of it and then I was disappointed when he didn't! My resignation speech only took nine seconds this time and then I collapsed into the chair in front of him.

What came out of his mouth next is a perception-based statement; don't judge him too harshly when you hear. He said:

'I was sure you were a lifer, I was sure we had you here for life!'

Interesting choice of words. During the next hour or so I explained my hopes and dreams for the future and why I wasn't going to be in the bank 'for life'. During the next month (four weeks' notice given), and because of my high profile role within the bank (training and developing people), the rest of the senior management team dropped by, whenever they were passing, to wish me well. They all said something different to my boss, but also perception-based. To a person they all said:

'We knew some day you'd be gone.'

'It's been written all over you for years.'

I felt like saying, 'well, someone could've told me! I'm lying awake worrying about what I'm about to do and your all acting like it was as obvious as anything.' At my going away party many people dropped by to wish me the best of luck and to 'say a few words'. I then heard things about myself for the first time, including what people admired about me. I was delighted and upset at the same time; how can you be in relationship with people for 23 years and the only time they tell you what they admire about you is when you're leaving?

Before You Go . . .

It seems to me that this is part of our culture: we can only tell people what we admire about them when they're leaving. When we've no option, no time, there may be no other opportunity, we finally tell them what we think. So the classic times are when you're leaving a job after 20+ years, when you're emigrating or, worse still, when you're lying on a hospital bed, there's a crowd around the bed and you've only got minutes left!

The Last to Know . . .

Since then I've made it my purpose in life to help others find out what's 'written all over them' *now*. You see, you are the same as me, you have unique talents and your ability is written all over you. And, as mentioned earlier, if you're not looking for it you won't 'see' it, your brain won't allow you to. And if you can't see it you think it's not there and doesn't exist – 'I'll believe it when I see it' – but if nothing changes you may never 'see it'. So don't be the last to know – let's find out what is amazing about you!

You'll see how to do this in the next Flying Lesson. In the meantime, however, there are a couple of other issues worth addressing first.

Motivated to Be Right

I believe that we have become too quick to blame 'lack of motivation' as the reason for someone not doing something. On the one hand, I'd like to think that the FLY exercise shows that perhaps you and I can't actually motivate another person; they'll still see what they want to see. So if we try to convince another person that something else is better and 'more right', all you then have is a row about who's got the best evidence, the best stories.

During my time in the bank there was a man working as a porter and part of his job was to sort the post every day that came into head office. While he was fundamentally a nice person he was also an 'energy vampire', that is, spend any time with him and you'll come away exhausted. Occasionally, though, I had to challenge him if some post was delayed or possibly missing. He would then become the most motivated and energised person in the bank. OK, I accept that his mission was to prove me wrong and defend himself, but he certainly had no problem being motivated.

Three Levels of No Parking!

Another example of this clash with motivation happened recently in my family. We decided at the last minute on a Saturday morning to go shopping since my son's football game and my daughter's hockey match had been cancelled. So off we went to the city centre in the car. Thinking of parking, I wanted to know which part we were going to. Angela mentioned which stores we would be going to and she also said where it would be good to park. I said (while still on our way) that 'there's no way we'll get parking there, those spaces go really early, but I'll say no more, let's see what happens'.

We get to the part of town that Angela wanted and guess what? No parking! My reaction? Delighted! I said there'd be no parking and lo and behold, no parking. There is a God after all! Now, if you think that's bad there are two more levels to this.

Next level: I'm quite happy now to tour the area showing that there's no parking. I'm actually 'looking for no parking'.

And Level 3 is: we come around the area for the fifth time and finally there's a parking space exactly where it would suit us best. I then say that 'there's someone else right behind . . . can't turn now . . . didn't see it in time . . . we wouldn't fit.' I'll find some reason why we can't park there!

The World Champion of Optimism and Motivation

Now don't you dare label me or judge me to be a negative, de-motivated, cynical, typical male car parker. I am the most motivated person you could meet, I am the World Champion. But I am also a human being who wants to be right, has a need to be right, from time to time.

No Negative People

So it turns out that there is no such thing as a person needing to be motivated. There is no such thing as a negative, cynical person.

The world is full of wonderfully talented, unique and motivated human beings who, from time to time, will channel their 'motivation' into being right about something, and if this is not convenient for you. . . . Too bad!

There is still something we can do about all of this, however, which you'll be glad to know I'm coming to in a moment, but I'm just tying up some loose issues here first and the next one is: What do people think of you?

The Need to be Right vs Personal Brand

So often we get concerned about what people think of us, who we are, our reputation and our 'brand'. And yet, I've shown above that it has already been decided in one second or less when the person met you first. To illustrate this allow me to use the example of you and your current boss. If you don't have a boss then you'll have customers, suppliers, even family members who the following will apply to but I'm going to use the 'boss example' because it's the easiest and most common. Please consider the following:

+ When your boss first met you he or she decided (at 250 kph) what type of worker and person you are.

+ From that moment on they just 'see' the parts of your behaviour that suits them, that keeps them 'right' and they ignore everything else. In fact, they don't see it, therefore it doesn't exist.

+ Your customers have done the same. They believe that you only offer two products, for example, when in fact you might offer 20. Although you are worn out telling them that you offer 20 they don't hear it and still think have to go elsewhere for the others.

So if your boss has formed a judgement of you, for the sake of this lesson let's say that it's an unfair perception, a limited view of who you are and what you are capable of, what can you do about this? What can you do about your customers' views? How can you change someone's perception of you?

The Six Forces that Shape Perception

The good news is that there are six ways perception can be challenged and/or changed. The first three can take awhile and they are Time, Distance and Energy. The second three can change perception in a blink of an eye, and they are Information, Behaviour and High Self-Worth. The following is an explanation of each one, but first remember what 'perception' is: perception is the meaning we give to an event or to information received.

Force # 1 – Time

'Time is a great healer.' Sometimes, given enough time, we will change our view about something or someone. Over time we will accumulate some of the other following 'forces' and eventually change our mind.

Force # 2 – Distance

One of the tricks of the FLY exercise is that you are too close to it. If you look at the FLY diagram from the other side of the room the word FLY is much easier to see. So if we can 'rise above' an issue we are struggling with, insert some distance between it and us, then we may see it differently, see it for what it really is.

Scientists studying chaos will tell you that there is no such thing. Sure it feels like chaos at the time but if you could rise above it you'd see that it's just old habits being repeated over and over.

'Coaching' is just another word for distance. When a coaching relationship has worked well what's really happened is that the coach has helped the client 'rise above' the issue and see it for what it really is. From this vantage point the client will come up with a much better, more elegant solution than is possible when being too close to it.

Force # 3 – Energy

When you and I are tired we have completely different perceptions than when we are in great form. Our solutions to our problems, our perceptions of what's possible for us, expand when we are in great form, physically and mentally. When we are exhausted we struggle to see anything of value, hope and inspiration.

If an organisation does a change management programme when everyone is tired, most people will have a poor, limited cynical perception of what the programme is really about.

When I'm tired and have to make dinner I look into the fridge and see nothing!

As I mentioned above, these three can take a little time. The following three strategies can change perception in an instant.

Force # 4 – Information

Information changes perception. The more you find out about something or someone the more likely it is that you'll change your mind, unless of course you'd rather not change your mind and 'be right' instead.

Have you ever changed your mind about someone? If we looked at exactly what it was that encouraged you to change your mind I bet it is because you found out something about that person that you didn't know.

So while 'more information' changes perception, the real issue is that you were 'open to receive' more information. Maybe you were caught unaware, your defences were down or maybe you were in a better mood. More about this is a moment.

Force # 5 – Behaviour

Behaviour changes perception. A new action or a change in existing behaviour works. This is the second best way to challenge and then change someone's perception of you. If you really want to show someone that they've got the wrong impression (perception) of you then you need to *do* something differently. Not only that but you will have to stick with the 'new' behaviour until it works. So persistence is also important here, more about this and mood shortly.

If you were to meet my former bank boss today he would tell you that his perception of me changed forever during that brief chat we had when I resigned that morning from the bank. So it took that action, that behaviour, to completely change his view of me. That's when he realised that:

'There's more to people than meets the eye.'

I know my leaving the bank after such a long time is a dramatic example. It doesn't always have to be like that, but it does have to be different, authentic and persistent. If when I offered my resignation he talked me out of it, and if I had changed my mind then, I don't think he would have changed his perception. In fact, my lack of persistence and follow-through would have confirmed to him what he already thought: that I was a 'lifer'.

Force # 6 – Mood

Mood alters perception. In fact, this is the best, fastest and most exciting way to change perception. This is so good that it actually deserves a Flying Lesson all of its own so I'm not giving you any information on this right now. Trust me, it'll be worth waiting for.

In Summary –

✪ Perceptions are **judgements** you make about people, events, situations and information and then quickly become **the need to be right**.

✪ The **pessimist** and the **optimist** are both right. So is the **cynic**!

✪ The need to be right is **emotional not logical**. In relationships it can be a form of violence toward another. At the very least it means that compassion and understanding have left the relationship.

✪ **Your brain finds** information that it thinks is important to you and filters out everything else.

✪ But, just because you can't see something **doesn't mean it's not there**.

✪ What else are you not **'seeing'** at the moment? What information is your brain not allowing in? How is it that your brain is unsure about what's important to you?

✪ Just because you can't see how you might be **a fantastic success** doesn't mean the clues aren't there.

✪ So, **be careful what you look for** because you'll see it.

✪ What is **written all over you right now** that you can't see but is really clear to everyone else?

✪ There are **six forces** that can cause a perception shift: Time, Distance, Energy, Information, Change in Behaviour and, the best one of all, a Change in Mood brought on by **a healthy dose of high self-worth**.

<u>The Law of Perception</u>

Change your mind and you change what you see.

What you look at actually changes before your very eyes.

The most limiting perception of all is our perception of ourselves. Change your mind about yourself and you change your world.

Warning: Don't limit your future to what you can see today, there's much more going on.

When You Know What You Are You'll Know What to Do

Now that you have decided to leave your comfort zone, succeed in the panic zone and manage your perceptions, you should now play to your strengths. In other words, every goal you set and action you take should be grounded in the strength and reality of your natural talent and ability.

Deal Breaker

I should warn you right at the start of this lesson that it contains an exercise that is wonderful and terrifying, inspirational and scary, easy and really difficult. This exercise could be a deal breaker between you and me. Just when everything was going so well . . .

Of course, this exercise is also wonderful for your self-worth and self-image as it creates a 100% accurate picture of what's fantastic about you and the unique talents and gifts you have to offer. It is perception-based and as such is always right!

From Design to Action

As you'll see, this Flying Lesson is divided into two parts. The first part is the Design Phase. This is where we will discover your talent and ability, and then we will proceed to the Action Phase to get things moving. The design phase can be quite creative and will be broad, strategic and all-inclusive. The action phase then is where we start to narrow the approach, ditch things that are not for you and really start to focus the effort.

Talent for Everyone

It has been proven by Marcus Buckingham and Donald Clifton in their wonderful book *Now, Discover Your Strengths*, using extensive and scientific research, that everyone has a talent for something. In fact, not only does everyone have a talent for something but they are, in effect, better at 'it' than are the next 10,000 people. This of course also includes *you*.

Your Blind Spot

So you have a talent for something and you are better at 'it' than thousands of other people! But the irony is that because you are great at this, because it comes easy to you, you are the very person to undervalue it. You assume everyone is good at it. And because you undervalue your ability other people do too, though they really admire others who can do what you do, even those who aren't quite as good as you!

Most people undervalue what they are and overvalue what they are not.

So if you don't value what you are, how dare you expect others to value it? Likewise, if a team of people working together in a large organisation doesn't value what they do, then how can they expect their colleagues in other departments to value it? In other words, they can't even sell the value of what they do to themselves!

Talent Rediscovery

So how do you find out? How do you discover or, as is usually the case, rediscover your natural talent and ability?

Well I guess it's always good to make a list, a physical representation of you talents. So you could sit down with a blank page and your lucky pencil, with a pot of tea and the 'good biscuits', and start a list. It is likely that the first line or two will be really difficult but as long as you stick with it the task should then get easier.

You could think back over the positive feedback you've received over the years (at least, I hope you've got positive feedback over the years!), however small, and include this in your list. As well as considering other people's feedback you can also include what you feel are your talents and abilities.

The 6 Clues

Another way to help you with this is to consider the following characteristics of someone who has discovered 'their thing':

1. The action, the engagement in the process, comes easy to you

2. You look forward to doing it

3. While you are engaged in the activity time seems to stand still; you experience that magical feeling that top sports people describe as being 'in the zone'

4. Or perhaps 'time flies' – you lose all sense of time and are surprised when you finally look at the clock

5. You experience accelerated learning while engaged in the activity – in other words, you learn faster and retain information longer than usual

6. Engaging in the activity itself provides you with enough reward and satisfaction – you'd do it for nothing.

Now, in case you are having a laugh, I haven't just described having sex! Although in another way I probably have, but you can't make a living from it . . . let's not go there (ever regret starting to say something?).

So, to how many things on your list can you apply these qualifying criteria? Or, before you write your list, how do these 6 Clues influence your choices? Do they help?

Anyway (in time-honoured fashion), put the book down now, 'move away from the book!' Do not proceed any further until you do a list.

Fact or Fiction?

Now that you've done your list the difficulty is that there is a fundamental flaw in it – the flaw is that the list contains both fact and fiction and we've no way of knowing which is which. Because each thing listed is based on your self-perception each one is 'right'. But, as we saw in Lesson # 2, we are not always as 'right' as we think. How do you separate out the fiction from the fact, the padding from the good stuff? Very simple but you won't like it.

You need to do the following exercise. This is the one I mentioned at the very start of this lesson and it could be the toughest or the most exhilarating thing I could ask you to do – we'll know soon.

Design Phase – The Talent Exercise

Welcome to the best exercise you can do for yourself. This is even better than a diet or a de-tox so do yourself a favour, commit to this and it will be the greatest gift you'll get this year.

Expert Panel

For this exercise you will need a panel of six people. Ideally your group should be made up of three people who know you from work (past or present) and three people who know you best from outside work (please avoid parents if you can!). Your panel does not have to be lifelong friends or colleagues – you'll be surprised by how well you are known by someone you've only met recently.

Two Questions

You will ask each of your panel members to reply to the following two questions:

> **Q1**: *'Please list the talents and abilities that you admire this person for. These are things that you've noticed that they do really well. These can often be so natural to them that they come easy, and they also may not be aware that they have these talents, abilities and skills.'*

(*Note*: You need to tell the panel members that we are not interested in compliments or 'nice' things said. We are only interested in specific information that has occurred to them over a couple of days. We are not expecting an instant answer to this.)

> **Q2**: *'Based on your answer to Q1 above, please now list the Dream Jobs on the planet that this person is perfect for right now. These can be anything that you feel build on their talents and abilities. You can even create the ideal job if you feel it doesn't exist right now.'*

You then thank them for taking part and let them know that their contribution to this exercise is a wonderful gift that you will cherish and use.

Worries

Yes, I realise that this exercise brings with it some worries right at the outset: Who do I ask? Have I got six people to ask? What will they think I'm doing? What will people at work think?

So let me address these concerns. Yes, I said that I'd like six people and they should be a mix of work and non-work and that's the ideal. But we can still get a great result without this ideal. Sometimes four people is enough (less than this gives us very little to work with) but eight or nine is too many.

Yes, a mix of work and non-work would be good but let's not allow that to ruin a good exercise so if you want to stay away from colleagues that's fine too.

Yes, four, five or six friends and relatives can still produce the desired result.

Then there's the issue of what to call this? How do you explain it? I recommend that you be totally honest and say that you are 'reading this fantastic book at the moment and this is an exercise you feel is worth doing'. Other people have told work colleagues that this is part of a 'Personal 360 Degree Development Programme' and would welcome their input.

But let me reassure you of one thing based on the hundreds of clients I have done this exercise with over the years: Your panel of people will be delighted that you asked them to participate. They will be honoured and will appreciate the importance and uniqueness of this exercise. In fact, when it's done they may ask you to do the same for them! I hope this happens because that means that the good work we are doing together is going beyond us. Someone else is benefiting from a wonderful exercise.

Case Study # 1 – Mags

To illustrate how this work can go beyond you and me the experience Mags had is a great example. She left it very late to do the exercise. In fact, it was the night before we were due to meet for our next coaching session. She was out with eight friends to celebrate something and Mags decided that she would ask them to help her with this exercise before the evening got going.

They were all sitting in a semi-circle booth in a night club and she waited until everyone had a drink in front of them. She then asked for their attention, explained what she needed and also added that all eight didn't have to give her feedback, just three or four would be enough. So the person beside her started with what she admires Mags for. As soon as she finished the next person spoke up without any hesitation. When she had finished the next person started. All the while this was happening others around the table were agreeing and making supporting noises.

At this point Mags had had enough. She thanked the people who had given her feedback, said she was very embarrassed by the whole thing and suggested they now carry on with the rest of the evening. There was a moment when everyone seemed to agree but no, the fourth person took up the exercise and gave her feedback. Mags had to wait until everyone had a turn before she was off the hook!

There was then a lull where everyone had a sip of their drink and thought about what had just happened. Then the person beside Mags said, 'OK, my turn' and off she went with everyone giving her feedback! In fact, this continued all night with everyone giving each person feedback and they had a great time. That's why I hope that the work we are doing together goes beyond us because . . .

What you do for yourself you do for others.

Case Study # 2 – Anne

Anne worried all the way home from our session about who would she ask to help with this exercise. But she decided that she wanted to start right away so she rang her mother for feedback – she could be the first person on her panel.

She phoned her mother, reminded her of the fact that she's working with a coach and told her about the exercise. She then explained that she'd be happy to get feedback from her as part of her panel. She then said:

> *'So Mum, please name one thing I do that you admire me for. One thing that I do really well in a natural sort of way.'*

There was a sudden silence on the phone, then eventually her mother asked:

> *'Why are you bothering with this life coach stuff? You seem to be just upsetting yourself with ideas like this. No Anne, I'll have to ring you back after some thought to name one thing you do really well!'*

Ever since then I have cautioned clients about asking family members to help with this exercise.

Case Study # 3 – Shane

Shane was the Head of Marketing for a very large organisation. He liked this exercise so much, 'and it was going so well', that he decided to ask 15 people!

He came back to me with all the feedback and started to read it to me. He told me what eight people had all agreed on, then another seven thought something else, and he carried on like this for awhile and then came to an abrupt stop – you could almost see a lightbulb go on over his head when he said:

> *'No one thinks I'm good at marketing!'*

There are always surprises with this exercise which is why it's important to touch on the following three scenarios:

Feedback Scenario # 1 – Some Overlap, Some Truth

You'll remember that at the outset of this exercise I suggested that you also do it; in other words, you should answer the two questions about yourself. What this allows us to do is to compare the results of the panel to yours. Or, to quote from Lesson # 2, compare your self-perception to others' perception of you.

Where there's an overlap that means your self-perception has been confirmed by the panel so therefore it is true. So most clients get this result; the overlap of agreed information shows where the truth is, and you can build your future work and career success on this truth.

Feedback Scenario # 2 – Much Overlap, Much Truth

I've also had many clients who have a large amount of overlap between their version of themselves and everyone else's. This just means that there's more information to work with. It doesn't necessarily mean that it's a better result than above because the real test, in fact three of them, has yet to come.

Feedback Scenario # 3 – No Overlap, Where's the Truth?

Occasionally I also have clients where there is no overlap between their self-perception and others' perception of them. Usually you can see this coming from the previous coaching session because when you explain this exercise to them they either get quite uptight about the prospect of it or they say that they've no idea what people are going to say.

At this point I would normally invest an extra coaching session or two in helping them develop their self-awareness which can alter their self-image. They can then start a new level of self-acceptance where they feel better about the feedback from the panel and are more motivated to use it.

The Top 5

We've now arrived at the point where each person of your panel has suggested a range of 'dream jobs' for you. Our job now is to reduce this list to the Top 5 options. That is, the Top 5 options that you feel most excited and enthusiastic about, that you'd love to spend most of your time doing and also getting well paid for it.

In fact, if you refer back to the start of this Flying Lesson you'll see the list of the 6 Clues. Here, we compare each option to that list to ensure that it has the right qualities.

By the way, we don't have to prioritise these five options; we just have to agree on what they are. Also, I have no difficulty if you want to have one wild card, something completely creative and impractical. There'll be plenty of time later to get practical and sensible but why not include something wild at this stage?

Action Phase – The 3 Tests

We will now apply three tests to each option. These tests firstly serve as a reality check – sometimes we can have a romantic view of something when the reality can be quite different. Secondly, the tests help us to gauge where you are with each option and thus give a clue as to the pace and work required to make progress on each one. The tests are, in order of difficulty:

Test 1 – Knowledge and Skills

Do you need to do some research to learn more about the area of endeavour before you get started? This can involve reading up on the subject and maybe taking a short introductory course first to test that it's for you.

Test 2 – Network and Contacts

Is there someone you know who is already doing 'it'? Can you arrange to talk to them and find out what you need to know before you get started? It would have to be something very unusual to avoid the '6 degrees of connection' that can help you find out what you need to know.

Test 3 – Get Started

Maybe you are ready to get going? Maybe you've just been playing a waiting game? So how about doing 'it' as soon as possible? And, by the way, I'm a great fan of doing 'it' for free first. If you really want to know if something is for you do it for nothing first and see how you feel afterwards.

Final Stage – Make Your Mind Up Time

So, to recap where we are now. We've identified three to five work or career options that you are excited about. Each option is already based on your natural talent and ability even before you get started.

We then apply the above tests to each option to improve your skills and knowledge, to get advice from someone already doing 'it' and then you should be ready to get started.

We have now reached the make your mind up time. Now this can vary from committing to the pursuit of something, to starting something or to leaving something.

It is always important to stay in a position of strength for as long as possible. In other words, let's not create any ridiculous high risk leap out of your current reality (comfort zone). It is important to get as much as possible in place first to ensure that the transition or change is low on worry and high on excitement.

Time to Fly

It took me 18 months to decide to leave my bank job after 23 years. However, during those 18 months I was also preparing for the day it may happen. The decision to leave the bank was one of the hardest things I have ever done, whereas actually leaving in comparison was one of the easiest.

Very often the decision to commit to something is the difficult part. What we then actually do and the actions we take can often be much easier than we thought, but I'm convinced that it is that initial commitment that holds most people back from following their dream. More on this in the next Flying Lesson but for now I'd like to tell you a client story that will illustrate everything I've covered above and has a twist in the tale!

The Landscape Gardener

He arrived into my office like something out of a business magazine: six foot four, thirty something, immaculate suit, shirt, tie, power shoes, power watch, power socks. He introduced himself and outlined his corporate career to date which was all highlights. So, you can imagine my surprise when he said that he wanted to be a landscape gardener!

I asked him to name three different types of roses and he said, 'red, yellow, white'.

'Two different types of grass?' I enquired.

He said, 'long and short'.

I said, 'you're probably perfect for this!'

I informed him that it's good to know what you want but (as you've seen above) it's not where you start. So I brought him back to the first step of discovering talent, strengths and abilities and suggested we do the panel exercise 'just in case'.

About four weeks later he had the results from the panel and we discussed them. They pointed toward a number of options within his corporate area that he could consider, and there were a couple of other suggestions that didn't particularly 'float his boat'. So when we agreed what the Top 5 options should be most of them were about different corporate possibilities, but we also included landscape gardening as he was still very insistent about it.

We then applied the three tests to each option and in the case of the gardening option I suggested that he make contact with his local gardener, find out where he was working, arrive with breakfast for him and his crew and ask him all about landscape gardening. My concern was that it could be 95% cutting grass and hedges and you might only landscape one garden a year!

He was up to this challenge, found a helpful and generous gardener and reported back with all he had found out. He then wanted to know what's next.

I said that he should now landscape a garden for free for someone. He took a week off work and landscaped his grandmother's garden for free. She told him what design she wanted, the plants and flowers she preferred and he went to work.

In the meantime he has been developing the other options too.

Finally it was 'make your mind up time'. He started by thanking me for putting him through the process. He said that he did things he never thought he would and as a result has found things out about himself that he never knew.

He said that he has made his decision and it is to stay where he is and look for a move to an area that he would enjoy more. But, he added (and this is the point of the story), that he is not going to wake up some day when he's 60 and wonder should he have been a landscape gardener. He said:

> *'What we have achieved in our work together is a* **no regrets policy** *and for this I am very grateful.'*

In Summary –

✪ Everyone has a **talent for something**; some people have more than one talent.

✪ In fact, you are better at 'it' right now than the next 10,000 people are – what could you achieve **if you really developed** this talent?

✪ Because it comes easy to you, **you are the very person** who most undervalues it.

✪ There are **6 Clues** that point the way toward talent and ability.

✪ The Talent Panel Exercise is based on the principle that **other people may know us better** than we know ourselves.

✪ The Secret to Great Work – discover what you are **good at** and then **get customers** for it.

When you know what you are you'll know
what to do.

Flying Lesson # 4

Confident Anyway

Everything I have covered so far is important and yet one of the magic ingredients of success is *confidence*. In this and the next Flying Lesson I'll be looking at two ingredients that are vital to success and yet have a magical quality too. In other words, they can defy logic. So get ready to go to the land beyond logic! My favourite quote about confidence is from Woody Allen:

'Confidence is what you have before you have all the facts.'

There is so much wisdom in such a short sentence. Confidence can be naive; it can be innocent of all the facts. Confidence is what you need when the challenge seems to be greater than your resources. Confidence is required to cope with the risk of the unknown or the challenging.

Confidence means trusting yourself to push past moments of fear and not give in. Very often you have to look bad before you can look good. The longer you wait to go after your dreams the less confidence you will have.

Both Sides of the Equation

Confidence is unique in that it exists on both sides of the equation, on both sides of the 'equals' sign. By this I mean that most elements of mental fitness that people strive for are simply natural outputs of smaller things working better. For example, 'motivation' is a result of smaller things working better. If there is a formula for motivation it could be X + Y + Z = Motivation where X could be Motive, Y could be Taking Action and Z could be keeping Self-Belief. I'm not suggesting that this is the definitive formula for motivation; I'm just using it as a quick example.

Other outputs resulting from smaller things are Success, Happiness, Calmness, Inspiration and Assertiveness. So I believe making these the issue is an incorrect approach to developing them further. No, we should break them down into their constituent parts, work on those and then see the natural result. Confidence, however, seems to be one of these parts and also part of the output.

In other words, you and I need some confidence to get going and then when we've taken action we get more confidence as a result.

So in this Flying Lesson we'll be looking at why confidence is vital for you to succeed even more. You'll also learn how to generate confidence quickly, create it when you need it and keep it longer than usual.

But first, let's start with what confidence is, and what it is not, before we look at how to have it easily and effortlessly.

Developing Confidence is about Taking Action

A definition I like is:

> *'Confidence is the ability to take appropriate and effective action, however challenging it may feel at the time.' – Rob Yeung*

So confidence is about doing what you need to do when you need to do it, regardless of how uncomfortable it may feel. This should sound familiar because now we are back to the comfort zone/panic zone from earlier in the book.

Keep the Faith, Dude!

Confidence involves some risk-taking because that is where the discomfort comes from – there is an element of unknown and yet you take action anyway.

The word 'confidence' means 'with faith' and faith usually runs ahead of evidence. Self-belief is a conditional form of confidence; it is dependent on seeing evidence that something is possible:

'I'll believe it when I see it.'

As I mentioned already though real confidence has to do with faith (not belief) and faith runs ahead of evidence:

'I'll see it when I believe it.'

If you refer back to Flying Lesson # 2 you'll remember the piece about 'seeing is believing', and while this form of conditional confidence is better than nothing it is totally dependent on, and derived from, evidence. Struggle to see or take away the evidence and you also take away the belief.

A 'Wait' Problem

So we can't wait for you to see enough evidence to help you believe in yourself so you can be confident enough to get started! No, confidence is about getting started anyway. Now, I'm not talking about being reckless, foolhardy or careless. I'm just saying that there may not be the right time, the right set of circumstances or the right person. It's time to take control back and take action.

The longer you wait to go after your dreams the less confidence you will have, and the fear that you'll never get what you want will become more intense. True confidence doesn't come from not having fear, it comes from trusting yourself to act despite your fears. The presence of fear just means that you have big dreams; and the bigger the dream the bigger the fear.

The following is my favourite example to illustrate the above.

The 4-Minute Mile

During the 1950s the world's best middle distance runners had made great progress in reducing the time it took to run one mile but the progress had slowed down and halted at about 4:04 and remained at this level for years. Despite all their hard work and training they could not get beyond this barrier.

At the time there were many articles published stating that it was physically impossible for a human being to run a mile in less than four minutes. In fact, in 1953 there was an article published in the medical journal *The Lancet* by an eminent physician who claimed that a human being would not survive running the mile in less than four minutes – the athlete would die in the process!

In May 1954, Roger Bannister ran the mile in 3:59:04 and did not die in the process!

During the next 12 months more than 20 athletes ran the mile in less than four minutes. Why? How could they suddenly do it? Well of course, they now had 'belief'. They believed it was possible because they had the evidence; they could see it and so believed it.

Confidence is Emotional Not Logical

But what did Bannister have? He had no evidence. In fact, he read that he could die in the process! OK, he may have had a new pair of the latest runners and an extra cup of tea with loads of sugar, but most importantly, he had *faith* and faith runs ahead of evidence.

Faith is emotional not logical. Confidence means 'with faith' so it is emotional too; it is a feeling rather than anything else. This means that becoming more confident can happen really quickly and easily but staying confident is the real challenge. This is what we'll turn our attention to now.

We'll start by looking at the three types of confidence and why each one is important. Then we'll explore the four stages of developing lasting confidence, and in particular we will use the Cycle of Confidence to kick start the process. We'll then end this lesson with some quick fixes, tips and strategies.

The 3 Types of Confidence

Now it is time to look closer at how to develop new levels of confidence in your life, work and sport. There are three types of confidence and it is up to us to be aware of, use and develop each one. The three types are Behavioural Confidence, Emotional Confidence and Universal Confidence. To be a genuinely confident person you need all three to be working well.

Behavioural Confidence is the one most people think of first. This is our ability to take action, to do things, to follow through on things, to keep promises and to take chances. **Emotional Confidence** is our ability to know our emotions and then express them without damaging relationships. The third form of confidence is probably the most important and is the spiritual component of being confident – **Universal Confidence**. It is about your ability to trust in the universe, in God, in Buddha, in Allah, in Karma, in Positive Mental Attitude. In other words, it is believing in something bigger than yourself when all else seems to be failing. Without this one working well it is very difficult to really develop the other two.

Do, Say, Trust

Simply put, behavioural confidence is your ability to *do* things, emotional confidence is your ability to *say* things and universal confidence is your ability to *trust* things.

Two Out of Three Ain't Bad

It is likely that at least one of the three may require some attention from you right now. Or, when times are tough you may revert back to being overly dependent on one or two and neglect the third one. I know that I am usually good at the behavioural and universal stuff; I almost always have a belief that everything will be OK if not better and I'm good at taking action. Emotional confidence is something I need to be better at.

But that is no problem because I am married to someone who is world-class at emotional confidence. Angela is of Italian extraction and wears her heart on her sleeve all the time. To say she has a 'short fuse' is something of an exaggeration. Angela doesn't do fuse! I know how she feels about me every moment of every day whether it is convenient for me or not. In fact, there are times when anyone within a ten metre radius will know. This is emotional confidence and while it can be scary to be around it is good to get me out of my emotional comfort zone.

So over to you: is there an area of confidence that you have neglected lately? Which one of the three are you strongest at? Which one could be developed? In relation to identifying areas where your confidence could be working better please complete the following statements:

If I was more confident I would do less of _____

If I was more confident I would say _____

If I was more confident I would trust that _____

The Real Thing

So genuine confidence occurs when someone is strong at all three of the above confidence areas. There is one other ingredient required which I'm coming to soon, but for now let's say that a really confident person takes action, follows through even if it's uncomfortable, speaks their mind without disrespecting anyone and has great belief, faith and trust that they will prevail.

The 4 Stages of Developing Confidence

For the moment let's move away from the different types and look at the stages of developing confidence. We will return to the different types again later. Please think of each stage of development as a step on a stairs. Each one is better than the last (a higher step) and gets you a step closer to the above mentioned 'Real Thing'. You see, it's all very well to say that you need all three working well but how do you achieve that in practical terms? This is what we'll address now.

Stage 1 – The Absence of Confidence

There are people who will claim to have 'no confidence' which of course is not true. It actually takes some confidence to say that you've none! (If you know what I mean). Everyone has some confidence even if it is difficult to spot. So the first level is to admit how much confidence you think you have and even search for some small amount to get you started. This way you have 'some' which is better than 'none'.

Stage 2 – The Illusion of Confidence

This form of confidence is better than the previous stage. It is called the illusion of confidence because it is has the look of confidence . . . but not really. This is someone pretending to be confident. This is the 'fake it until you make it' approach. Let's face it, it's better than nothing, and does actually work on occasion, but it is also exhausting. It is like having to regularly psyche yourself up for something. It will only work for as long as you have the energy to do it. Again, it is better than nothing and people may actually 'buy it', but to you it's more like role playing and you will feel like an impostor.

Stage 3 – The Creation of Confidence

This is better than an illusion of confidence. This is where some results are coming through and is also known as 'confident because … getting results'.

But if stage 2 is dependent on creating and maintaining an illusion of confidence, and stage 3 is dependent on getting results, then both of these are external to us and are effort-full. The best form of confidence therefore must be internally created and be effort-less.

Stage 4 – The Presence of Confidence

This is the best form of confidence. It is effortless and not dependent on maintaining an illusion, nor does it require results to keep it in place. It is effortless because it is a presence – it is more about 'being' than 'doing'.

This is a form of confidence that is great to be around; it is infectious in the best possible way. It makes other people feel good about themselves without actually doing anything. It is also the presence of Leadership.

Therefore this form of confidence is also what this lesson is called – it is … Confident Anyway! It is the ability to feel confident despite how results have been.

It is also where the above three types of confidence come together with one other magic ingredient which we will explore in the next Flying Lesson. To take the practicalities even further, we will now look at some confidence tricks that are designed to get your confidence growing quickly and easily. In other words, how to move quickly through the above four stages.

Confidence Tricks

The Confidence Loop

This is about taking immediate control of what you do, think and feel. It's clear that what we do, think and feel is linked in a continuous loop. For example, if you feel nervous about an event you will tend to behave nervously, think nervous thoughts and thereby continue your feelings of nervousness about this type of situation or event. So if you let your feelings get the better of you, you will create a self-perpetuating loop that reinforces the fear and reduces your confidence.

However, if you think differently (change your perception and then your mind about something), you'll start to feel differently and then you'll start to behave differently. So the great news is that you can start anywhere you like with this; enter the loop at any point with a change and the positive knock-on effect is inevitable. The following are some suggestions.

Give Your Confidence a Jump Start! Quick-fire Strategies Designed to Spark the Loop into Life

DO – One of the most consistently successful con tricks of all time continues to be the 'act as if' trick. This is designed to take advantage of the fact that there is a direct link between mood and body language. It's now clear that how we stand or move has a direct effect on our mood and attitude at the time. If you want to generate more confidence quickly, then adjust your posture quickly – stand, walk, talk, smile like a really confident person and, as you've seen in the earlier lesson on perception, people 'buy what they see'. It doesn't matter if you are churning inside; present your-self as a confident person and people will believe it. In fact, if you can keep it going you will start to believe it too!

Now I accept that this can be hard work but all we are look-ing for here is a jump start; there are other things you can do too. Remember, it is easier to act your way into a feeling than to feel your way to action.

Public speaking example: If you are about to give a presenta-tion to a group of people and you are feeling really nervous, act as though you are really calm, confident and in control. Use your body to calm your mind and the audience will accept it. You can collapse in a heap later when they are gone!

THINK – Here we can just refer back to the earlier Flying Les-son on perception: change your mind about something and you start to see it differently. When you start to see it differently you'll start to feel differently about it and then you'll behave differently too. The best ways to change our mind are:

1. Find out more about something – the more information you have the more likely you are to change your mind about it.

2. Find ways to re-frame the situation. Can you look at it differ-ently? By applying a different label or definition does this help you to see different possibilities?

Public speaking example: Don't try to 'sell' the audience or convince them of anything. Just tell your side of the story; give them your knowledge and information and let them make up their own minds. Find out more about the audience and make your talk about them, not about you. This is not a speech, a lecture or a sales pitch – this is about you illustrating your product/service with some stories that the audience will like and enjoy.

FEEL – Borrow confidence from some other experience you've had. You see, if you were a client of mine I would expect you to have a list of what I call the Top 10 – the top ten presentations you've given in recent years, the top ten sales you've made, the top ten tournament wins, the top ten birdies, the top ten goals you've scored and so on. I would expect you to have these recorded somewhere and then be able to produce and read this list when you need a confidence boost. I refer to this as 'borrowing confidence' and again, it is as great way to fire the loop into life.

Close the Loop

So to summarise this part, I expect you to have a level of self-awareness and self-management so that when you feel that your confidence is low and needs a quick start you will now use the Do – Think – Feel technique to fire your confidence and quickly change your state of mind. There is another area of confidence and self-belief worth mentioning now that can also transform performance – placebo beliefs.

The Placebo Effect – Mind Over Matter

The placebo effect is very commonly encountered in the world of pharmacology. Various experiments have shown that, in certain situations, when given a pill containing no drugs whatsoever a volunteer patient will still exhibit a positive a physical response to the 'drug' if they believe that it does contain chemical elements that are beneficial to their condition.

The power of the placebo has nothing to do with the pharmacological properties of the drug; its effect derives from the entirely false belief that the drug is effective. Anything that can create an illusion of credibility will reinforce this is the mind of the patient, strengthen their belief and by implication the drug's effectiveness.

It does help that the drug is administered by a doctor wearing a white coat with a stethoscope though!

Packaging and pricing can also tap into this placebo effect. For example, aspirin in fancy and attractive packaging are more effective than those in dull and plain packaging. Research has also shown that cheap painkillers are less effective than more expensive ones. The belief is that if it costs this much it must be really good!

The key point in all this is that the power of the mind is exercised through the medium of belief, and it doesn't matter if the belief is true or false – all that matters is that the person believes.

You'll now see a link here between this idea and my earlier one that 'Universal Confidence' is our ability to believe in something bigger than ourselves. This is similar to that concept.

So, it's important to generate a placebo belief or two. A belief that helps to keep you going which may not even be true but helps you to be really effective.

One of the most remarkable findings of recent psychology is the fantastic capacity of human beings to mould and shape evidence and information to fit their beliefs, rather than the other way around. It is our capacity to believe in something despite the evidence, and sometimes despite our other deeply held beliefs, which separates top performers from the rest.

These people have learned that beliefs are not just aimed solely at the truth, but at what works. They have taught themselves to 'crank up' their optimism at the point of performance, to shape the evidence (their perception) to fit their beliefs.

Invent a Placebo

To discover a new placebo all you need to do is invent or create one. And to do this all you need to do is change a belief. And to do this all you need to do is change your perception. So it is open for everyone to take control and create something that may not be true but can help you to be incredibly effective. It may not be that easy but it is worth the effort. There may be times ahead when all you have to keep you going is faith in something that may not even be true, but if it works, helps you to be more confident today and it doesn't damage relationships . . . why not!?

I'd like to share with you a couple of my (many!) placebo beliefs. The first one is a golf one.

When I am playing golf and have hit my first putt on the green two or three feel past the hole, as I'm walking to take the next one I always announce to the group (aloud, to increase the pressure on myself to try harder):

'I always get the one back!'

And guess what – I (usually) do!

My business example is that anytime I speak to a group or at a conference I always get follow-up business from someone in the audience. So 'speaking' is my best 'sales' strategy and … it is!

I'd like to end this section with my favourite placebo effect story which illustrates all of the above.

The Doctor

Once upon a time there was a small town doctor who was totally devoted to his patients and the well-being of his town. And when he had some spare time he channelled this dedication into researching a specialist form of patient care. He became such an expert in this field that he was invited to present his findings to a very prestigious medical conference.

He travelled to the city the day before, checked into his hotel, had a nice meal and settled himself comfortably in his room. One of the important facts about this doctor is that he only ever prescribed drugs or medication for his patients when they really needed them. Otherwise he always explored other ways of helping them become well again.

However, on this particular night, and against his better judgement, when preparing to go to sleep he took a sleeping pill as he was very anxious about the conference the next day. He then lay back on the bed and had the best, most relaxed and refreshing sleep he'd had in a long time.

The next morning he awoke easily just before the alarm went off, swung his legs out of the bed and sat upright on the edge of the bed marvelling at the great sleep he just had.

He happened to look at the bedside locker and there sitting on top was the sleeping pill, and missing from the locker was the small shirt button he had found on the floor of his room the night before!

In Summary –

✪ There are **three types of confidence**: Behavioural, Emotional and Universal.

✪ To develop behavioural confidence, **do something now** that you've been avoiding lately.

✪ To develop Emotional Confidence **express something now** that you've been holding on to.

✪ To develop Universal Confidence look for an order to things that may seem random; find a way to **trust in something bigger** than you.

✪ There are four stages of developing confidence which involves moving quickly from the **absence** of confidence to the **illusion** to the **creation** to the **presence** of confidence. The secret is to keep moving, keep doing, keep recording successes, keep celebrating them and keep calm about the whole thing.

✪ There is a continuous confidence loop which involves **Doing**, **Thinking** and **Feeling**. You create the doing part by changing and improving your body language and posture. You create the thinking part by reminding yourself of past successes and in this way borrow confidence from other areas. And finally you create the feeling part by 'acting as if' you are really confident.

✪ **Invent and cultivate a placebo.** This may remain a secret to you or you may wish to make it a public belief in yourself to help keep the pressure to perform. However, when you go public you are creating the possibility that others will remind you that the belief is not actually true (which of course is the whole point).

Confidence ER

In case of emergencies please try one or all of the following:

✦ **Big Smile** – it changes the chemistry of the situation

✦ **Walk Tall** – regardless of your actual height make a stand for yourself

✦ **In the Eye** – look everyone and life in the eye, you've nothing to apologise for

✦ **Uncross Your Arms** – open up your body language to let someone in

✦ **Smile More** – as above

✦ **Dress Up** – wear clothes that make you feel good

✦ **Say So** – don't harbour resentment, get it off your chest

✦ **Thank You** – make an extra effort to thank people

✦ **Sharing is Caring** – share these tips with someone else, especially children.

Confident People

Confident people respect and understand themselves, and continue to observe as they grow and move through life. They know what they want and they are not afraid to keep setting goals and challenges. And, they tend to be solution focussed and don't feel overwhelmed by problems.

We Feel Good in Their Company Because . . .

We know where we stand with them whether they are feeling good or bad. They don't depend on putting down other people in order to feel powerful therefore we can trust them to be fair. They can be lively or quiet, peaceful and relaxed because they feel that they do not have to prove themselves.

The Feather

I'd like to close this Flying Lesson by relating a story that shows how innocence and placebo can be great allies in our efforts to build our self-confidence; sometimes we just know too much!

I was sitting in my favourite chair at home reading the newspaper trying to ignore my four-year-old daughter as she was playing about me. Apparently then she decided that she wanted to fly. She explained to me that 'if teeny tiny birds could do it and because she's such a clever girl with a much bigger brain' surely she could do it too? So she climbed across me, my lap, my newspaper and got on to the arm of the armchair. She got upright into a standing 'ready-steady-go' position and then leapt out up and then down.

She admitted afterwards that this attempt was not entirely successful. Using her 'huge brain' she then remembered something. She galloped off out of the room, up the stairs to her bedroom and back down the stairs like a herd of small elephants. She arrived into the room with the feather that we found in the local park the previous day. She climbed across me, my lap, my newspaper and got on to the arm of the armchair. Clutching the feather very tightly in her little fat dimpled hand she went for it again.

She told me triumphantly afterwards that the feather definitely helped!

Flying Lesson # 5

The Value of Self-Worth

A therapist might define self-worth as: how capable and lovable you feel you are. As I'm not in the therapy business the definition I like to use is: self-worth is the quality of the relationship you have with yourself. In other words, how you feel about you, right now. I am about to outline the affect this has on your relationship with others and with life in general.

Highs and Lows

If self-worth is how we feel about ourselves then it is likely that this can change from moment to moment. Depending on how we deal with challenges, disappointments and success our view of ourselves is likely to be affected from event to event. So to illustrate how self-worth works I like to suggest a scale of 0 to 10, 0 being low self-worth and 10 being high self-worth. It should be stated at this point that low self-worth is perfectly normal and part of being human. Also, there is no such thing as a 1/10 person, but there certainly is 1/10 behaviour or mindset or attitude. Also, 10/10 is perfectly normal and human too, but more about this later.

2/10

Let's start with low self-worth. I'm going to call it 2/10. When you and I are 2/10 we are fed up, negative, pessimistic and tired.

We don't see how we are making a difference to anything or any-one, we feel like nobody cares about us, we allow people to mis-treat us and we feel cut off and isolated. As mentioned earlier, this is all perfectly normal. These behaviours and attitudes also impact on our discipline, in other words, we lose our structure, our routine and our good habits. When you and I are low we don't keep to the diet, we don't keep fit and what's more – we don't care! We lose our discipline, lower our standards, blame everyone and everything and quickly become helpless. The attitude is one of, 'what's the point, who cares, who knows, it wouldn't change any-thing anyway'. We sell ourselves short, we settle for less, we don't ask for what we are due and allow others to behave the same way. But remember what we're talking about here: the quality of my relationship with myself. Here's the affect that 2/10 has.

Radiation and Attraction

When we are in 2/10 mode that's what we are like to be around. In other words, I only have 2 in the tank therefore it's all I have to give to others. Since I can't give what I haven't got, if I'm not motivated I will not motivate others. If I can't give to myself, I can't give to others. When we are low we are radiating at a low frequency. This radiation frequency is important because it creates a kind of magnetic attraction. For example, when you and I are having a 2 day we will attract to ourselves other people who are also at 2! And of course we get on great with each other because we share the same limited, cynical view of life and business; we are on the same wave-length.

But that's not all. Not only do we attract people of a similar disposition but we will also attract events, situations and possi-bilities. But they will only be 2/10 possibilities! You don't land a 10/10 opportunity when you're having a 2/10 day! They go else-where that day. So it's radiation and attraction, or cause and effect, whichever you prefer, but by choosing to ignore these laws we are choosing to ignore vital feedback.

Role-playing and Quick Fixes

Having said that, there are a couple of strategies that we can use to by-pass the above. The first strategy is role-play. In other words, there are times when we pretend to be higher than we are. We are a 2 pretending to be a 9. We will attempt this in certain situations or with certain people. Or we will attempt this when we are low and are looking for a quick fix. However, role-playing has a price: it is exhausting, it fools no one and usually afterwards we are lower than when we started. For example, someone at 2 pretending to be at 9 for a meeting will actually be at 1 after the meeting. They will hate themselves even more for pretending to everyone that they are fine. It is a hollow, impostor-type feeling.

The second strategy is to look for quick fixes. These can range from indulging in behaviour or habits that are not good for us, things that have nothing to do with self-respect but provide a temporary high or a short escape. A particular form of a quick fix in life today is – being busy. Very often when we are low we can generate a form of worth from how busy we are. In fact, we have a need to be busy because that creates an illusion of being needed, being vital. But the challenge comes when we are actually not that busy – take away busy and you take away worth. Self-worth has very little to do with what we do but everything to do with who we are.

Please permit me again to state that feelings of low self-worth are normal, human and particularly Irish! So that's not the issue – the issue is how long we accept feeling low rather than doing something about it.

Now let's look at high self-worth.

10/10

When you and I are at 10 we are a joy to be around. And we don't have to be comedians or the 'life and soul of a party' to be 10/10. Instead we are a calming, inspiring, encouraging, compassionate presence. The following traits also then come naturally to us – assertive, enthusiastic, energetic, motivated and passionate. These are all natural outputs of 'worth' working better. We are radiating 10 and of course attracting others who are at 10 as well. Genuinely confident people love the company of other confident people. Not just because they share the same outlook (which they do) but also because they need to challenge each other to reach new heights, in exactly the same way that 2s need to comfort each other! Also, when you and I are at 10 we attract 10/10 opportunities and possibilities. In fact, the reality is probably that we are creating them or at least seeking them out.

When we are at 10 we insist on high standards for ourselves and others, and our discipline is so good that it doesn't even feel like discipline. We are good at 'selling ourselves' without having to feel like we have something to prove, were looking for a favour or trying to please people. We feel strong and we encourage others to feel strong. At 2 motivation is a problem, at 10 we've gone beyond motivation and are looking for inspiration. At 2 we talk about 'team morale' but at 10 we are more interested in 'team spirit'. So I guess the obvious question is: how do we get from 2 to 10? And beyond!

Give by Example

An important point here is that it is difficult to provide self-worth to someone else. You can tell someone they are the most amazing, wonderful person you've ever met, but if they are at 2 at the time they will find many reasons and examples to not believe you. So I can't give self-worth to you and you can't give it to me. I can't give it to my children and I should not expect them to make me feel good about myself. You and I can't get high self-worth from an organisation simply by turning up and expecting the boss to give it to us! Of course, we can still offer something, in fact two things:

✦ We can live our lives consistent with someone who has wonderful self-respect and self-worth, and

✦ We can inspire, encourage and support others to do the same.

Two Choices

When you and I are at 2 we have two choices – a toxic one and a healthy one. Let me deal with the toxic one first. In my travels in the corporate world I have met so-called 'leaders and managers' who have taken the toxic choice, which is rather than doing something about their own low level of worth, they devote all their time and effort into pulling everybody else down to their level. This is not a healthy form of leadership.

So let's look at the other choice which or course is, 'I'm at 2 and decide that I can and want to be better. How do I get from 2 to 10?' The answer is that it is simple but not easy, especially when you are at 2 to begin with. But the solution applies to any number in fact. So regardless of whether you are at 2 or 11 the strategy is exactly the same, but in both cases it starts with a decision to change, a call for action, a positive intention.

Action! (with Good News)

As with most things the decision to change is usually the hardest part. In this case it's the decision to aim higher, to improve and to get our act together. Following this it's time for action but it should be noted that when we are at 2 we should not attempt an action that's at level 9! At 2 we're just about able for a 2.5 thing. What are these magic actions? Why you know already! They are all of those small but important things that we've been putting off lately. We're looking for anything that is important to us personally or professionally that we've been avoiding, even though we know we would feel good about ourselves once we've attended to it. In other words, it's something that we know we should do but it may be a little uncomfortable or may involve a stretch from us.

The good news is that you can get from 2 to 10 in about three leaps. This does not have to be a miserable journey of small steps forever. And, like confidence, it tends to develop a momentum of its own. It just requires a small regular injection of disciplined behaviour.

The Greater Good

As mentioned earlier I also believe that what we do for ourselves we do for others. By this I mean that there is a transformation that takes place where self-worth becomes team-worth, group-worth and also company-worth. The more individuals that take responsibility for their own sense of worth the higher the frequency of the organisation. So what I do for myself I do for others. Also it means that you have a contribution to make to my sense of worth and confidence. Now we are in the business of Team Spirit.

You can create an 'Igniting Purpose' by starting with some 'Igniting questions'. Here are some of those questions:

'In your life or career are you "settling for less" at the moment?'

'Are you allowing someone to take advantage of you?'

'Is there a discipline, hobby or leisure activity that worked really well for you in the past that you could return to?'

'If you really, honestly had high self-respect is there anything you are currently doing that you should stop doing?'

'If you really, genuinely valued your career is there anything that you could do more of? And less of?'

The Mental Fitness Workout

Introduction

Self-worth is the quality of the relationship you have with you. How you feel about yourself today or even right now. The health and vitality of this relationship will determine the health, vitality and energy of all other relationships.

So, how to get from 2 to 10 on the scale? Follow the recommended weekly challenge of this workout. Note the Hazardous Waste Warning but keep going and you will easily and effortlessly move from 2 to 10.

Recommended Weekly Intake

✦ Select any three of the following strategies and complete them within the first week.

✦ Then, at the start of week two pick any three from the remaining ones and go again.

✦ Then at the start of week three repeat the dose.

I can guarantee that if you follow this program your self-worth will be alive, energetic and bouncing around the room! Prepare yourself for some exciting opportunities!

Hazardous Waste Warning

The creator of this program cannot be held in any way responsible for the levels of happiness, success, health, vitality and fun that may occur if you exceed the above recommended levels or continue beyond the time frame. Please note that overdoing the above will be extremely hazardous and dangerous for those of you wishing to shrink and play small.

Of course, if you do wish to remain as you are or feel that this may be a waste of your time then start this program but give up about half-way through the first week – that is guaranteed to result in further shrinkage.

Self-Worth Strategies

✪ **Create a better self-image**. Low self-image creates low self-worth. So start to appreciate something about your appearance. Look for something that you can like about yourself, however small it may be. Your favourite toe, a beautiful fingernail, five eyelashes, anything to get you in the mood. As you start to appreciate your body more, your self-image will improve and so will your self-worth.

✪ **Give away some old clothes**. Our clothes form such an important part of our image. Are you holding on to some clothes that you haven't worn and probably never will? Why are you keeping them? Maybe you're waiting to grow back into them. However, in the meantime they constantly remind and torture you about who you are not and what a failure you are! Let it go! Let them go! Give them to charity, throw them away, have a ceremonial burning of the 'old you'.

✪ **Look-good-feel-good syndrome**. You know those clothes that you keep for just 'special occasions' and you love to wear because you know you look great in them – take them out and wear them tomorrow to somewhere ordinary. Look a million dollars at the supermarket.

✪ **Take time for you**. Do something just for yourself. You're already world-class at giving to others so now give to you. When you invest time in yourself in this way you are recognising that your needs are as important as everyone else's and so you increase your self-worth.

✪ **Do something you've got to do**. Think of something important that you know you need to do but you keep putting off. It must be important though. Not some trivial nuisance thing but something that will add value but you've been avoiding. Now do it! I can guarantee that you will feel great, bursting with energy and then you may be confident enough to tackle the real thing that you've put off!

✪ **Make an assertive phone call**. Time to make that call to ask for something that is really yours anyway or to complain about something. Now's the time to do it and a quick tip is: stand up when making this call. You will be naturally more assertive and hopefully on the other end of the line they will be sitting down!

✪ **Eat well for half-a-day**. By this I mean the second half of the day. Let's say afternoon and evening. If we put the wrong sort of petrol into our car it won't fire on all cylinders, the same applies to our bodies. Eat well and drink loads of water. This is a great way to boost self-worth.

✪ **Say what you mean for one hour**. For only 60 minutes say exactly what you mean and stand well back! Don't edit, sugar coat or be overly protective of others – go for it. As self-expression improves so does self-respect.

✪ **Ask for what you need for one hour**. For only 60 minutes ask for exactly what you want and what you need. This is a sign of strength not weakness. It is also the best way to get what you want.

✪ **Express your appreciation to someone.** This is one of the greatest boosters we can give to our self-worth. Give credit where it is due. When we show our appreciation for others we help them with their self-worth. What we give out we get back so it helps us too. It does not have to be a grand, massive gesture (of course these are good too).

✪ **Grasp a new experience.** Do something different, something you've never done before. Sign up for a pottery class, eat different food, visit a new place … the possibilities are endless. When we do something for the first time we experience a change in energy and learn something new about ourselves.

✪ **Listen for an evening.** Spend an evening listening to everyone rather than talking. This approach will change the focus of your evening and will take you 'outside' of yourself. Even listening to a radio programme or music that you wouldn't normally listen too will help you practice. Listening is becoming a dying art because we've no time to listen to everything. Due to the pace of life today our attention span is reducing. We are a country of great talkers; does that make us poor listeners?

✪ **Start exercising.** Regular exercise is a booster shot of self-worth and is one of the easiest ways to gain confidence in our bodies and also our abilities. You will really feel good about yourself when you take exercise. You'll think better, be more creative and solve problems easier. Start small and doable, focussing on quality not quantity and build from there. Also, pick something you like that suits your rhythm and your vibration rather than following someone else's suggestion.

✪ **Forgive someone.** Forgiveness does not mean that we allow anybody to do anything to us, forgiveness is about letting go. If I cannot forgive you then my angry thoughts will keep me wired to you. When you truly forgive you set yourself free. How can you be high in self-worth if you hate someone? By the way, just thought I'd share this with you – 'resentment' is when you keep taking the poison hoping the other person is going to die!

✪ **Breathe deeply for 15 minutes**. The way we breathe affects the way we think, feel and act. Calm the body and the mind will follow. Slow and complete breathing oxygenates the system, removes the build-up of toxins in the body, lowers your heart and pulse rate and your cholesterol levels, and boosts your immune system. You are aiming for six to eight breaths per minute.

✪ **'Act as if' for one hour.** For one hour, using your posture and body language, act as if you are really confident, really calm or really successful. This could be the way you walk into a meeting or into a social event. If you want to be assertive you must stand assertive. It is easier to act your way into a feeling than to feel your way to action.

✪ **Say 'NO' once when you really want to**. Stress happens when your mouth says 'yes' and your gut says 'no'. This is about being true to you more often, about putting yourself at the top of the list occasionally. Surely you deserve this?

✪ **Congratulate yourself**. Any chance you get give yourself positive feedback. Develop your own personal success culture. Anytime you do anything well acknowledge it before you rush on to the next thing.

Please note that the above strategies are not 'rocket science' – given a few minutes you would have come up with these too. The 'rocket science' is actually doing them!

It is also worth stating that the idea of this programme is to gently stretch you out of your comfort zone. For you to realise that by making small changes to your daily routine you can end up with huge changes to your relationship with yourself and with life. So don't get competitive about this! It's not about winning or losing, it's not necessarily about how many you get done. It's about the fact that the objective of life is growth not comfort.

> *'Your playing small does not serve the world; there is nothing enlightened about shrinking so that other people won't feel insecure around you. As you let your light shine you unconsciously give other people permission to do the same. As we are liberated from our fear our presence automatically liberates others.'*
> *– Marianne Williamson*

So it turns out that what you do for you, you are also doing for others. That means that investing in your self-worth is the most unselfish thing you can do. This program is the best thing you can do for yourself and others this year!

> *Have fun with it, be kind to yourself and get slightly uncomfortable as often as possible!*

Flying Lesson # 6

Goal-Setting is for Wimps

I hope we are all agreed that when it comes to achieving something having 'a plan' is a help. It doesn't have to be a rigid, carved-in-stone, obsessive/compulsive plan though because flexibility is important. Things can change so the plan should probably respond to change too. But having some plan for success to refer back to regularly is a good idea. And typically this is where 'goal-setting' usually appears.

Now I like goals, I love them in football for example, but it's the way we've been taught to set them that is the problem. So in this Flying Lesson I'm going to highlight the problems with the typical goal-setting approach, explain why goal-setting doesn't work for most people most of the time and outline in detail a better approach that will work for most people most of the time, and which for some will be life-changing.

SMART Goals

This is the most used goal-setting model today. The letters usually stand for Specific (S), Measurable (M), Achievable (A), Realistic (R) and Timed (T). In other words, your goals, your achievements, your aspirations should satisfy each of these requirements. It should be very specific, nothing too woolly or loose – so 'to be more successful' doesn't measure up, not specific enough. There should be clear measurements along the way and the end result should also be measured so you know when you've got there; so 'to earn more money' isn't measurable so it won't work. Wanting to be 'the most successful person in your country' at something is not achievable and realistic if you're not particularly gifted. And finally, 'sometime' has no deadline therefore is not timed.

So, 'I'd like to be more successful and earn more money than anyone else sometime in the future' is not a goal as it doesn't satisfy the above criteria. In fact, I'm not sure what it is – maybe it's a wish.

The Difference between a Wish and a Goal

I guess the main difference between a wish and a goal is that a wish is woolly, non-specific, has no measurements or deadlines and no plan to achieve it. But it's worth saying that a wish is better than nothing and, in terms of achievement, a goal is better than a wish.

But on the other hand there is something romantic and magical about a wish. I'm thinking back to my childhood and how I'd love it when someone would say 'make a wish' following the breaking of a wishbone or throwing a coin into a fountain. And I'm thinking of all the great children's movies and stories about 'wishes coming true' or 'to wish upon a star'. So let's not discount 'wishes' too quickly in favour of goals, and we will return to the topic of romance and emotion later.

SMART is Too SMART

Now it's time to discredit this form of goal-setting. I can't wait any longer. In fact, I'm breaking out in an allergic reaction because I've already mentioned SMART more than I want to.

Fatal Flaw # 1 – Projects not People

SMART goal-setting actually started out life as a model for short-term project management. If you want to deliver a project in one to two years' time then you better make sure that it satisfies all of the criteria mentioned above (don't ask me to spell it again, the rash is getting worse!). The result should at the outset be very specific and easy to communicate; the steps and stages should be measurable and let's go for something that is realistic and achievable within that time scale. But that's the first fatal flaw: it's for projects not for people, and it's only for a year or two whereas most people's hopes, dreams and aspirations are for a longer period than that. So, it's brilliant for projects and terrible for people.

Fatal Flaw # 2 – Logic is Boring

It's all very logical isn't it? It's all very dry and sensible and rational and reasonable. SMART doesn't contain one emotional word. It's all a bit too 'left-brained' and devoid of creativity and emotion. Where's the passion in the model? Surely the passion to succeed is a vital part of achieving anything. So, it's brilliant for sensible projects and terrible for a level of achievement that will require passion, guts and risk.

Fatal Flaw # 3 – Realistic is Comfortable

If I can bring you back right to the start to Flying Lesson # 1 for a moment: 'realistic' is too close for comfort to the Comfort Zone! So making the end result realistic means that there's no rush. No need to get started too soon, let's wait until things are better and, any way, are you ready for this? If you never take a step forward it doesn't matter because you're not that far away from it anyway! So, 'realistic' is part of the trap of 'comfort'.

Fatal Flaw # 4 – What is 'Achievable'?

I feel that I could write a whole book on this question alone, and maybe some day I will because how does someone know what is 'achievable' for them? I guess the person would look back into their experience, assess their ability, predict their future prospects and then decide what they should set out to achieve and what they should forget about. In other words, 'achievable' is probably achievements to date plus 10%! However, based on my 23 years working for a bank it is not 'realistic' and 'achievable' that I am doing the work that I do now. If someone had told me about two years before I left the bank that I would be doing what I do now, I wouldn't have believed them, it would have been 'unbelievable', but it has happened. I'm sure we can all think of people who, despite modest upbringing and education, have achieved beyond 'achievable'. So, achievable is still too close to comfort and way too limiting.

Fatal Flaw # 5 – Goal-Setting is for Wimps

The very inclusion of the words 'achievable' and 'realistic' mean that this goal-setting model is for people with low self-worth – the 2/10 mindset I mentioned in the previous Flying Lesson. When you and I are in 10/10 mode we don't settle for going after something that's achievable and realistic; it doesn't inspire us to get out of comfort and keep trying. When you and I are low on the self-worth scale not only will we be reluctant to set goals, we'll even challenge the notion of goal-setting in the first place – let's call this 1/10 mindset. Then, when things start to lift, say from 2/10 to 4/10, we'll set some goals but they'll be of the SMART variety. However if we work at our self-worth and wait until we are in 8/10 or even 10/10 mode then we'll set some amazing and exciting challenges for ourselves. So SMART goals are designed for people who have settled for less than they are worth and are capable of.

I could keep going but I guess that's enough of the fatal flaws for now. I'm hoping that you agree or are at least open to an improvement, and if that's the case it's time you heard about John Naber.

The John Naber Story (so far)

In 1972 John Naber was watching the Munich Olympics on television. I was too. Unfortunately these Olympics are mostly remembered for the killings that took place of Israeli athletes but they are also remembered for other reasons. Mary Peters of Northern Ireland winning a Gold Medal in the Pentathlon. Tiny Olga Korbut in the gymnastics and also for the controversial basketball final between the USA and the USSR.

This was at the height of the Cold War between these two nations – relationships could not have been worse and now they had to face each other in the basketball final. The Americans, traditionally dominant in basketball, were leading by a point with one second left on the clock. The Russians called a time-out. After considerable confusion at the scorer's table, when the teams took to the court the Americans did not see the lone Russian player standing on his own directly under the American basket. The Russians simply threw the ball the length of the court to the unmarked player who made the easiest basket to win the gold medal. I couldn't sleep after watching the excitement of this match. The Americans, believing that serious officiating errors had been made, boycotted the medal ceremony and did not accept the silver medal.

Anyway, there was another reason John Naber and I were watching TV: an American named Mark Spitz was swimming in numerous events and it was rumoured that he would win everything. We were well rewarded because Spitz won seven gold medals breaking seven world records in the process.

Naber was watching Spitz win his seventh medal and said to himself, 'wouldn't it be nice to win a gold medal, to be an Olympic champion'? So Naber states that he started to dream of being an Olympic champion and then discovered a way to convert his dreams into goals. 'Yes motivation is important,' he said, 'and a lot of kids have motivation to be great and I'd like to be great too, but, I also have the way to do it.'

The background is that in 1972 John Naber could swim the 100 metres backstroke in 59.5 seconds. Watching the final live from Munich he saw Roland Matthes (not Spitz for a change!) win the Olympic final swimming a record time of 56.3 seconds. Naber continues the story: 'While Matthes was getting his medal I got a notepad and pen and did a quick calculation. We now have the new record time of 56.3 and, looking at the previous three Olympic winning times to establish the form and pattern, I estimate that the next Olympic winning time in Montreal in 1976 will be 55.5 seconds.

Immediately Naber realised that he was four seconds off the winning time (59.5 minus 55.5) calculated by him. So the 'dream' was now measured as 55.5 seconds. It's worth mentioning at this point that 100 metres is just two lengths of a swimming pool and to improve by four seconds in that short distance is a huge challenge. But, undaunted, he employs the following system:

✦ A four second improvement in four years works out as **one second per year**.

✦ He will train 10 or 11 months of each year so that's **1/10th second per month**.

✦ He will train six days a week so that's **1/300th of a second per day**.

✦ He will train from 6.00 to 8.00 am and from 4.00 to 6.00 pm every day so that's **1/1200th of a second improvement for each hour in the pool**.

So in other words:

1/1200th of a second faster in the pool in each training session = Gold Medal.

A blink of an eye is 5/1200ths of a second.

Naber continues the story: 'For me to stand on the side of a pool and say that during the next hour I only have to be a fraction of a blink of an eye faster means that I have a Believable Dream – I can believe in myself. I can't believe that I'm going to drop four seconds by the next Olympics, but I can believe that I can get that much faster today. Suddenly I'm moving, I've switched off the TV, and I'm going to the pool to train.'

In 1976 at the Montreal Olympics John Naber swam the final of the 100 metres backstroke in a record time of 55.49 seconds setting a new world and Olympic record. He went on to be America's most decorated athlete at these games winning four gold medals and one silver. Four years earlier he was watching TV with me!

John Naber's legacy to us is two-fold. First is his process of turning dreams into goals in three steps:

✦ Step 1 – Dream

✦ Step 2 – Performance Measurement

✦ Step 3 – Daily Process.

You see, the daily process must be very realistic, achievable and attainable; you have to do it almost every day, but don't make the dream itself 'achievable' and 'realistic'. 'Dream' is an Emotional Intelligence word, it's not logical and nor should it be. But the logical side of your brain doesn't like the word 'dream'; it's too loose and fluffy. But, too bad, because there's nothing wrong with it emotionally.

Referring back to the earlier part of this Flying Lesson and the SMART model I must say that I'm all for S, M and T. I love a 'specific' objective, I like to know how I'm doing so 'measurement' is good, and God knows we all need deadlines from time to time. But, I'll say it again: we need to get beyond 'achievable' and 'realistic'.

Now I believe that you can apply the John Naber approach to anything from happiness to business success to sport success to financial success. But' it's not important what I think. What do you think? Any problems with this approach?

Well the two main challenges I get at this stage from an audience are as follows.

Challenge # 1 – 'OK, let's see you play next week for United!'

Firstly, I don't want to play for United! But secondly, and more importantly, I can think of at least 20 physical reasons why I won't play for United. And that's the first point: in terms of human achievement I'm not just thinking of physical achievement; I'm thinking of being a success in the broadest terms. For example, I believe that everyone can be really successful in business if they adopt the above approach. I've no idea what the business is or their role in it, but apply the above process (with one condition which I'm coming to soon) and you will prevail. So when it comes to human potential, mental strength, motivation, confidence and resilience, apply the above and anything is possible.

Challenge # 2 – 'Naber was already a good swimmer'

This is absolutely true. Before he set out on his gold medal dream and quest he was a great college swimmer and could swim the 100 metres backstroke in less than one minute, but hold on, that's the whole point of the story and that's why I'm going to add an extra layer to the John Naber system.

X Factor

Let me refer you back to Flying Lesson # 3 about human potential. During that lesson I covered the proven fact that everyone has a talent for something. So yes, John Naber knew what his talent was – he was born to swim. The he applied his process every waking hour for four years. This means that the model now looks like:

✦ Step 1 – X Factor (your natural talent and ability in one area)

✦ Step 2 – The Dream (based on the reality of proven talent)

✦ Step 3 – The Performance Target (specific and measurable)

✦ Step 4 – The Process (the daily 'baby step').

When Naber had his daily target of 1/1200th second faster he improved quickly and efficiently early on. But there were also days when he felt he didn't improve, but each time he had his plan to go back to. Some days the daydream of being the Champ was enough and some days the tiny improvement was enough.

So, if you are prepared to re-discover your unique potential (if you don't know it already) use it, apply Naber's process and *you can't fail.*

You will be working in the exact arena that you are meant to be in and you will be applying yourself to full commitment each time you turn up. . . . Can't miss. I don't know how long it may take, and that may be where you will be tested: patience?

Neil's Dream # 2

In the last Flying Lesson of the book I'll mention my first dream and what happened, but I'd like to also share this one which I think works well here.

When I was still working in the bank and with no opportunity to leave I did however start to dream of some day being self-employed and doing what I do now – speaking and working with business, sport and life audiences. So I started to look for the first step (I hadn't come across Naber's story at this stage). I then heard a global conference speaker talk about the importance of reading and self-education.

He mentioned the following, totally un-provable, statistic: If you read every day for 30 minutes on one topic – it clearly must be a topic that you've a considerable interest in – then in three years you will be a national expert and in seven years you will be an international expert of that topic. I liked the sound of this. Now you have to understand that up to that point I only read about one book per year, usually something trashy while on holiday.

But I liked the sound of this. It didn't seem too much to ask and would be an easy way to become an expert! So, having a mild interest in human potential at the time, I went to the local bookshop and asked for whatever book was selling well in the self-help personal development area. The shop assistant recommended *Feel the Fear but Do It Anyway!* by Susan Jeffers.

I brought home Susan's book, sat down with a pot of tea and with my daily target of reading for 30 minutes, I read for about nine minutes! I thought this was really good and I left it at that – you don't want to peak too early! The next night, seven minutes, the following night, 11 minutes, the night after that, five minutes . . . eventually I got up to 30 minutes per evening and before you know it the book was finished.

Sitting here now in my office as I write this I am looking at hundreds and hundreds of books on one topic only – human potential – that I have read and I always have about two or three books on the go at any time. If he had said, 'In the next twelve years you have to read 1,300 books on one topic only' I would not have listened or thought it possible. But he didn't, he just said the 30 minute thing.

*Never, ever underestimate the power of daily
commitment in an area that you love, that comes easy to
you and that you excel at effortlessly.*

Apply Now for that Vacancy . . .

Let's now look at applying this to your work, sporting pursuits or life in general. You will need to revisit your thoughts and findings on your unique natural talent and ability that surfaced during that earlier Flying Lesson.

Depending on how you are feeling right now and where you are today on the self-worth scale you may struggle to come up with a dream that's big enough and exciting enough.

You may get the dream down but struggle with the performance measurement of it. No problem, write down the dream anyway and then stay open to receiving some signs, help or guidance over the next few days. But, and I can promise you this, you will not receive any help if you do not actually write the dream down.

Remember, I stated right at the outset that none of this is carved in stone. You are free to change and adjust as you feel you must. Whatever you have just written above should most of the time serve you well. There will be times when you are low and what you've just written will annoy you. You'll even question what your mental state was when you wrote it! But that's OK, that's normal too. Just be gentle with yourself, reassure yourself that when you wrote this you meant it. Then take care of yourself, work back towards 10/10 and then revisit it.

Step #1 – Please list here what you feel is your unique talent and ability

_____

_____

_____

_____

Step # 2 – Based on this what could your dream be?

_____

_____

_____

_____

Step # 3 – What measurement would help you to keep focus and know you have achieved the dream?

_____

_____

_____

_____

Step # 4 – What realistic daily baby-step will you take until the dream becomes a reality?

_____

_____

_____

_____

_____

Of Course, There is Also the Spiritual Option

The above model (Naber's approach) will work and is designed for people who liked the SMART model and perhaps are ready to move to something a little more inspiring. To other people it may still seem too logical, too contrived and does not leave room for some greater power to intervene. For those people I now offer the following slightly different approach:

✦ Step # 1 – Your X Factor

✦ Step # 2 - Your Dream

✦ Step # 3 - The First Step.

The more spiritual or universal power approach says that it is still important to have a dream, aspiration, end result and all you need to get started is the first obvious step. After that trust that the 'how' will appear. In other words, take one step and the next step will appear. You'll find that people who like this approach tend to believe in coincidence being a sign, being an intervention from a higher power – so this approach depends on your attitude towards spirituality.

The Road is There

This is a bit like setting out on a long car journey at night. You have to accept that the car's headlights will only light up about 200 metres in front of you. But, when you cover those 200 metres the next 200 will be shown to you. So the road is already there and you just have to trust that it is.

The Indiana Jones Approach

I'm reminded of that great scene in the Indiana Jones movie called *The Last Crusade* with Harrison Ford and Sean Connery. Picture this: they are in a desperate situation, they are trapped on a ledge and a vast chasm separates them from the ledge they need to get to. Sean realises something from a prophesy and shouts to Harrison (Indy):

'Take a step and the bridge will appear'.

Sure enough when Indy steps forward there is a bridge that was hidden by an optical illusion and they cross safely. I can also now explain the optical illusion by referring you back to Flying Lesson # 2 – A Word in your Eye and the information on Perception:

'Just because you can't see something doesn't mean it's not there.'

Coincidence: Destiny Calling or Just Plain Maths?

So where are you with coincidence? Some people feel it is a greater power showing the way and other people feel that it's just law of averages, probability or pure randomness.

By coincidence I mean those strange goose-bump things that happen, some are small and some are big. The small ones might be:

✦ You think of someone and one minute later they ring you.

✦ You've a song in your head and when you turn on the radio the song is already playing.

I guess the bigger ones are:

✦ You've decided to change jobs and you instantly see an ad for the perfect job for you.

✦ You're struggling with some issue and you are then introduced to someone at a social event who can be a great help with your dilemma.

So are these random things or are we being 'taken care of' or, better still, did we do something to help create this event happening? Did my thinking about a friend encourage him to ring me?

The Law of Coincidence

I happen to like this approach to achievement too. In fact, I use Naber's model for the financial success of my business and I use this more looser universal power approach for my really big dreams. I like coincidence and I regularly feel that someone is watching over me. I am especially aware of this when I'm down.

Almost every time I start to spend a few days doubting myself something happens to restore my faith and, yes, it does seem to happen every time!

But I have a Law of Coincidence which states the following:

When a wonderful coincidence presents itself you must act on it.

You can't waste it, you can't assume it'll come again. If you meet someone in a random way who can be a great help to you . . . you must ask for their help. Maybe it's a test of your commitment and by not acting it will be viewed that you're not ready yet, and let's face it, we're always ready for something wonderful.

Neil's Coincidence # 2

I would like to illustrate the above with an example of coincidence from my life. I have many examples that I could share but for now I'd like to relate this one.

I was booked six months in advance to speak to a large business audience. I felt that it was going to be a stuffy affair so I decided that I would try to liven it up bit. At that time the Irish singing star Brian Kennedy had a wonderful song out called 'Get On with Your Short Life' (it's still wonderful by the way). So I decided that

I would play this loudly as the audience was entering the auditorium. Now I knew there were royalty issues with playing music to a public event but stick with me for now. This was before 'downloads' were available so I had to go out and buy the CD. I went to the local music store and was told, 'you're in luck, only one CD left' (Good sign!).

Over the next few days while playing the CD I came across another wonderful song called 'The Reason We're Here' which would be perfect to play at the end of the event. So, I'd no idea what I was going to talk about but I've got the two songs I need! Then genius struck: why don't I ask the man himself to sing acoustically the two songs at the start and end of the event?! Maybe he'll like what I'll be talking about, enter into the spirit of the thing and not charge too much!

I got his website from the back of the CD cover and attempted to log on to get contact numbers. But, each time I got error messages or messages saying that the site was down. After a few days of this I decided that maybe it was a step too far and I should just settle for playing the CD. That night going to bed I had one last go, I offered up a prayer for help that went something like this:

> *'If anyone up there is listening I would like to get in*
> *touch with Brian Kennedy. Thank you.'*

The next morning, literally 12 hours after my prayer, I was walking out of a book shop in Dublin city centre and who do I almost bump straight into but Brian Kennedy! I stood there stunned. He was as close to me as you can get without actually touching! So ... I followed him down the street! (Remember the Law: you must act). He turned into a clothes shop, I followed him in. He was looking at sweaters when I marched straight up to him.

I hadn't thought about what I was going to say and unfortuneately what came out of my mouth next was, 'Hi Brian, I've been following you!' His expression changed from pleasantly surprised that a fan would approach so confidently to a look that said that his stalker has actually trapped him in the corner of this store! On seeing this I managed to blurt out the whole story and he relaxed. We had a great chat, he explained that his website was down at the moment, gave me his manager's phone number and said that if he's available he's love to do it, that it was a great idea.

Unfortunately, he wasn't available and rather than play his CD illegally at the event I told this story instead!

Don't tell me this was just a random event, don't tell me he was in that street at that time every day and it was easy to meet him. I asked for help, I got it and I was ready to act on the help I got. I have many more examples of this but I'm keeping just one more for the last Flying Lesson.

Make It Happen or Let It Happen?

So that's it, that's my personal approach for the really big things in my life. I prefer to let things happen and enjoy the journey along the way. Acting on intuition, gut feel and coincidence are the ways I get out of my comfort zone. And sometimes you just have to adopt some serious self-discipline to help the process along. Writing this book, for example, was my test for self-discipline.

In Summary –

✪ Having **a sense of direction** is important and it's better than nothing.

✪ **Goal-setting is a help** with applying structure to a sense of direction.

✪ **Structure** is important because it makes sense and is easy to remember.

✪ The **SMART** goal-setting model is the most widely used today with S for specific, M for measurable, A for achievable, R for realistic and T for timed.

✪ However, this was created for project management **not for human achievement**.

✪ To improve on this model you must include some **Emotional Intelligence**.

✪ John Naber's model does this by including the **dream** as the starting point.

✪ I've improved Naber's model by making **natural talent and ability** the starting point.

✪ The only part of a goal, dream or aspiration that should be 'realistic' is the **first step you take**. Everything else should be so big that the thought of achieving it makes you excited.

✪ There is a **spiritual approach** that says that if you know how to achieve your goals then your goals aren't big enough. Think big and then just start with the first step.

✪ Trust that the **'how'** will appear. **Ask** for help, say **yes!** to coincidence and **act** when you know you must.

Flying Lesson # 7

It's Your Time to Fly

In the previous Flying Lesson I talked about the importance of having a dream and I mentioned my dream of one day working outside the bank and that my starting point was reading. This was momentus for me because I only ever had one dream previously and that is what I'd like to share with you now.

Neil's # 1 Dream

When I was a ten-year-old growing up in Ireland, like many other children my age, I was playing every sport I could. I was playing Gaelic football and hurling for the school and outside school I was playing soccer for the local team and loving it all.

Then, one day, my father brought 'golf' into the house for the first time; he had just joined the Howth Golf Club. I was intrigued by this game and at 11 years of age I started caddying for him in Howth. However I should point out that Howth GC is very hilly and for the caddy it seems that every hole is uphill!

Anyway, I was now a caddy. Then at twelve years of age I hit my first golf shot with my first golf club. I can remember it exactly and from that moment I was 'bitten by the bug'. I loved golf. I soon started to dream of playing golf for Ireland as maybe any young Irish teenage golfer does. I was in school at class dreaming of golf, I was waking up at night time dreaming of representing my country. By the way, in each dream my father was caddying for me pulling the biggest, heaviest golf bag I could get! I could imagine the fairways lined with spectators all cheering everything I did. In my dreams I was holing putts to win many times; in fact, in my dreams I never lost!

Then at 17 years of age I was picked to play for Ireland on the Irish Junior Team. We travelled to Scotland to play in the Home Internationals; my dream had come true! The next year I got a great coach for my swing, I watched my diet, I got fitter, practiced harder – but was never picked again.

You are reading about the original 'one-hit-wonder' of Irish amateur golf. At the time I blamed everyone else – my club for not supporting me, my parents, Golfing Union Officials and so on. Looking back now though I know exactly what happened:

I had stopped dreaming.

Not only that, I felt an entitlement to my place on the team. How dare they! I also got too logical and neglected the emotional side of performance, the importance of having a dream and not getting into realistic, achievable logic. I was the first person ever from Howth Golf Club to represent their country. All I had was a made-up mixed bag of golf clubs, a commitment to practice and a dream.

I know that my heroes today are still dreaming: Padraig Harrington (golfer), Brian O'Driscoll (rugby player), Mary Robinson (global peace ambassador), Dalai Lama (spiritual leader). These are people who also have a made-up mixed bag of tools, a commitment to the work and a dream; they've never let go of the dream. You and I shouldn't either.

Who Do You Tell?

I hope by now your resistance is weakening and you are considering having a dream again, so the next issue might be: who do you tell it to, if anyone?

It's important to note that our family members are protective of us and don't want to see us get hurt or disappointed, so for this reason they will want us to stay safely inside our comfort zone and not aim too high. You may feel very strongly that your family is different and that's fine, you know them best. But generally speaking, they are protective rather than supportive, realistic rather than adventurous; this does not help us.

So Who *Do* You Tell?

I do think it's good though to tell at least one person what your dream or dreams are. It helps to clarify something when you have to vocalise it, when you have to describe it to someone. I think it also helps to hear it too! I'm lucky in that I have a number of like-minded people with whom I can discuss things like this. They will challenge it, challenge me, but they won't add to the doubts that I already have – they encourage and support me which is a great help.

However, going back to the goal-setting model outlined earlier, it could be useful to tell many people the process step, the small, regular daily step. Hopefully you can get away with not having to explain the whole thing and a simple statement very casually stated such as, 'ahh some day I'd like to . . .' may be enough. I guess it boils down to the fact that each one of us will need help with some part of this so it's asking for the help in the form of support that is the important bit.

Strategically Placed

I think it's important that when you have a dream that it is written down somewhere. Not only that, I'd like it written somewhere where you keep seeing it. But, following from the thoughts above, it should probably be still private to you. So a note on the back of a small card in your wallet or purse is one suggestion. A note on the inside of your bedroom wardrobe door is another good place. In other words, place a reminder somewhere where you come across it regularly.

Not only is it a reminder to you but it also works on a subconscious level; it is training your subconscious mind as to what is really important to you on a daily basis. And as we've seen in earlier lessons, once the subconscious understands what is really important it will set about helping you see this and find this in your everyday travels.

Some of my clients like to get really creative here; they like to create a collage that represents their 'dream'. So they will watch out for magazine pictures, headlines in newspapers, and even three dimensional bits and pieces like fabric, golf tees, paper models etc so that the collage of their dream exists in 3D form. Again, they would then position this somewhere semi-private so that they don't have to keep explaining it. This is probably even more effective than just a list, but either one is better than nothing.

1998

So in 1998 after 23 years working in a bank I started to dream again. I committed a few notes to paper in the form of the Dream Job and a Dream Life. I had no idea 'how' it was all going to happen but I did get clear on what I wanted and started to get clarity on what I had to offer.

At that time I was very involved in training and developing people in the bank. In fact, I should go back a little earlier and say that in 1990 I was plucked from obscurity within the bank to help set up and run the Training Department. I didn't want this, thought it would be a disaster from a career point of view, but I was given no choice.

However, three months into the job I was loving it. I couldn't believe my luck. I was skipping into work each day like you would when you were going to do your favourite hobby or pastime. By the way, back to perception for a moment – this was a real case of someone else seeing something in me that I couldn't see.

I performed at this level for eight years, got promoted three times, and along the way I occasionally received some very positive feedback.

You know how it is in large corporate organisations: you don't get much positive feedback but when you do something wrong you know about it straight away. It's a culture of assume you're doing a great job unless you hear otherwise!

But in 1997 I started to talk at home about the possibility of leaving the bank and doing something different and better with the skills I had acquired.

Angela and I had just moved house and were very stretched financially at the time. Now I'm talking about leaving my secure job and risking it all so, and rightly so, Angela got nervous when I brought up moving on. Anyway, it came up for discussion every so often and was also mentioned by a great friend of mine who was still in the bank but about to leave also. Ian wouldn't leave me alone on this issue.

Broke My Heart

Then it happened. Something happened in the bank that broke my heart. And it wasn't about money, promotion, bonus or anything; I'd got all those. Let's just say that I got a glimpse of what the future might hold for me if I stayed in the bank and got really upset. I arrived home to Angela and for the first time in about 18 months Angela said:

> *'Right, that's it, they don't deserve you, they don't value you, let's go for this, we'll live on bread and water if we need to, time to go.'*

And that Monday night in 1998, we made the decision that it was time for me to go. At 40 years of age I started on my CV, as I never had to do one before, and in the following five Friday business supplements of the newspaper there was a job advertised each week that I was perfect for! Coincidence or what!

So I applied for them all (act on coincidence). In the following weeks I found myself at the final interview for one and still in the race for two others: 'People are actually interested in me?!' I announced one evening.

If You Could Choose …

At this point it was very exciting. My confidence, self-belief and self-worth were rising by the day, and this is when Angela chose her moment (another Monday night by the way!) to say:

> *'I'm delighted for you, you're getting a great response, but, rather than react to the job ads, if you could pick someone to work for who would it be?'*

Without a moment's hesitation I mentioned a training company, run by a great guy called Conor O'Connell, that I had used many times to deliver inspiring programmes in the bank. Angela then suggested that I ring Conor and ask for a job!

I am a very independent person, and in particular I am terrible at asking for help, but asking for a job was totally out of the question, which is what I told Angela that Monday night. I was able to back it up with my belief that Conor probably wasn't looking for anyone, he certainly wasn't advertising and no, I'm not going to do that. Let's stick with the current opportunities.

But her suggestion got to me so the following Friday afternoon I slipped into one of the offices in the bank's corporate headquarters, closed all the blinds, darkened the room and rang Conor (this is before mobile phones by the way).

Conor knew who I was immediately as we already had a great working relationship and although I was speaking in code about why I was ringing he said:

'I don't believe this, you're asking me for a job now when I've just had lunch with my accountant and we've just agreed, like in the last hour or so, that I should take on someone new, and you've just rung me! Are you free to meet tomorrow?'

We met the next morning (Saturday), agreed a deal there and then, and I resigned from the bank on Monday!

The Hardest Thing and The Easiest Thing

The decision to leave the bank was the hardest thing I'd ever done; actually leaving the bank was the easiest. Angela and I spent 18 months on the decision to leave and less than one weekend on actually leaving. So I believe that the commitment to do something can be much scarier than the action you then take.

The commitment to put your faith in something – and remember I had no products, all I was selling was myself – is often the scariest thing to do, but of course for that reason it is the most rewarding also.

The Tom Cruise Moment

I think there's always got to be a leap of faith; take a step and the bridge will appear. It's like Tom Cruise in one of his many action movies – you'll have to leap from one train to another. The train you are on is your current set-up, job, work and so on. But can you develop another train quietly in the background? It may take a while before it even leaves the station. But with regular oil checks and plenty of fuel to build momentum it will eventually get close enough to your current train for you to jump from one to another (end of strained metaphor!).

So these are the learning points from my story of career change, but there is one other that is important and can even be dangerous.

The Wrong Way to Get the Right Help

At the start of this piece I talked about having my heart broken. But when I look at that in more detail I realise that the incident that happened was my idea in the first place! So you could say that I found something to help me make the decision.

So if you and I are struggling with a decision, as I did for about 18 months, we can enlist some help with this. If we are not strong enough to make the decision we will, even on some subconscious level, get help from elsewhere. When I look at the last six months of my time in the bank, and before my heart was broken, I had become a handful to manage. I also started to behave out of character. So I was testing the system, testing the organisation – on the one hand to see what I could get away with and on the other hand to bring the situation to a head.

I believe that in certain situations we will almost sabotage something so that it reaches closure at some point. We will bring something to a head so that a decision is inevitable. In a way this can be dangerous – dangerous for a relationship and for someone's identity. It is a very high risk way to get a decision made. In my case it worked fine and nobody got hurt but that isn't always the case.

If you feel you are acting out of character at the moment so you can test something or someone, maybe it would be better for all concerned to focus on making a decision and committing to something rather than the alternative.

The Power of Positive Expectation

OK, so you've revisited your natural talent and ability, you've got a believable dream and you've figured out the process bit, that is, your daily step or even just the first step. And you've created a visual representation which you have placed strategically where it catches your eye regularly.

You're almost ready to take off – maybe you have already? But there's one final piece of the plan and that is attitude. By that I mean having an attitude or a mindset that keeps you going and helps you to be a success magnet. What should that attitude be?

To illustrate this I'd like to relate a true story from my sport coaching experience. By the way, if you are not into sport, if it does nothing for you, that's OK. In fact that makes you a mature and fully functioning human being! But stick with this story; I am confident that there will be value in this for you too.

A number of years ago I got a phone call one evening from a guy who introduced himself, said he was at a recent golf psychology talk I gave and wondered if I could give that talk to his football team?

'Gosh,' I said. 'Are they that bad that you want to try golf psychology?'

He went on to say that he thought that the golf talk had tips and suggestions that would easily cross over to football. This was all news to me; I'd never considered this.

But, like anyone else I could feel the tug of the comfort zone. So I told him the truth which was that I've never worked with football teams and 'if he doesn't mind I'd rather not this time, thanks'. He was very insistent and I was weakening and then he mentioned what they could pay for a one hour session. Suddenly I was brave, gracious and available! So we agreed that we would 'do the talk' a week later one evening after their usual training session. We also agreed that he would collect me from my house, bring me to the club so we could have a chat on the way there and a post-mortem on the way home afterwards.

So the evening arrived and as I was putting my flip-chart into the back of his car, he said:

'By the way, we used a guy like you last year and he was awful!'

I 'thanked him' for this and said that I notice he didn't tell me this on the phone. He said that he's only telling me in case it comes up and he's sure that I'll be fine. I would've liked him to work harder at reassuring me; I was already nervous and this didn't help.

On the way to the club he told me that the team had just won the first round of the knock-out championship. They've never won it before but he felt that 'he was on to something with these guys, these are a special bunch'. We arrived at the club and while they were finishing their training session I was in the meeting room doing my best to manage my nerves.

Finally they arrived into the room, 25 of them, every one of them bigger than me, and they stood at the back of the room rather than come forward to the seats. Not only that, but using body language they sent me raw open hostility; clearly they did not want to be there. So I panicked and started editing my script thinking suddenly that some of it was a bit too emotional and maybe it could be more macho?!

Just then a voice got through my panic and it must've been a deceased footballer somewhere who sent it to me:

'The best form of defence is attack. So go for them!'

So I did. I said, in my loudest, most intimidating voice I could manage:

'Can you come forward please? I'm looking at the time, I want to get started, I don't want to be here all night!'

All I succeeded in doing was scaring myself. They took their time, the back row filled first then the second last row etc but two guys marched all the way up to the front without breaking eye contact with me. They sat in the two chairs closest to me and as they were sitting down one said to the other, just loud enough for me to hear:

'He even looks like that f**king fool we had last year.'

I heard this and thought to myself, OK, the gloves are off now, it's time for action. The best form of defence is still attack and since they were all sitting their with spoilt-brat faces and mumbling to each other, I said:

'Good evening, my name is Neil O'Brien and I have absolutely no interest in your sport!'

The mumbling stopped and all eyes were on me, which is what I wanted, and I proceeded with:

'Based on what I've just heard in the car on the way here, I'm gonna start with two questions. I have a plan for my talk this evening but I'd still like to start with these two questions.

'Question number one – what do you want from the championship this year?'

At this point the biggest human being I have ever seen stood up, he must've been sitting on three chairs! With pure hatred in his eyes because he thinks he has just been asked the most ridiculous question he said at the top of his voice:

'We ... want ... to ... win!'

And then he sat back down on his three chairs. Unfortunately, because I was really nervous, and I've just been threatened, an interesting thing happened to my voice and my breathing. My mouth had gone completely dry, I had brought no water to sip, I couldn't seem to get any oxygen into my system and my voice came out high-pitched with a warble in it for good measure. I am now sounding like the greatest wimp they have ever met. Anyway, with no voice I carried on:

'That's great, good to hear, anybody else want to say something?'

His twin brother got out of his three chairs – you could tell by the energy in the room that they could smell blood now – and he roared:

'To be a success!

'Great,' I said still searching for some voice that I could project. 'Anybody else?' And they all chorussed together as though it had been rehearsed:

'No!'

'OK.' I limped along:

'Question number 2 is – what, however, do you expect
is going to happen?'

The big guy didn't stand up this time and very quietly he said:

'A good run in the competition.'

I said, 'anyone else?' and his brother said:

'A high finish.'

I asked if anyone else wished to add anything. No one budged. I wasn't trying to set a trap for them, I wasn't trying to trick them. I just wanted to see how they would react to the different questions. But, as you can see, they've changed their answer. I got my voice and my breathing back and, as attack is the best form of defence, I then said:

*'You guys require major mental surgery. This job could
be too big for one person, I'm not sure if I have the time
and energy for this, because . . . you've changed your
answer.'*

I told them that all the other teams that are left will give exactly the same answers except for two or three teams. They will say 'Win' and 'Success' in answer to both questions, and we'll have to find a way to beat them.

*'Because, you don't get what you want in business, life
or sport. You only ever get what you expect to get.'*

They weren't happy with me and didn't trust me. I carried on with my script for the remainder of the session and got my lift home. The coach was thrilled, but I was concerned. Anyway, the next weekend they won and a month later I was back in to talk some more. The next time they won again and I was back again.

This went on until they reached the final for the first time in 20 years. And with five minutes left and the score tied, they ran out of expectation, backed off from winning, the other team scored a goal and that was it.

The following year I was back working with them again. They got to the final beating the winners from last year along the way and not only did they win the final but they won it for three years in a row. I now have 25 great friends and we still talk about that evening, the power of positive expectation and how it breaks down into the following requirements:

✦ You must expect to be a success

✦ You must expect a lot from yourself

✦ You must expect a lot from the people around you

✦ You must tell them that you expect a lot from them and,

✦ As often as possible, you must match your behaviour to that of someone who expects to succeed.

You will never get from life, business and sport what you want – that's your ego talking. You will only ever go as far as your expectation will allow. This is what I mean by having an attitude that keeps you going and helps you to be a success magnet.

As we approach the end of this journey I have kept a true client story for this moment. This actually happened and I think encapsulates most of the lessons contained in this book, so sit back, read and enjoy.

When Jimmy Met Barbara

Out of the blue one evening I got a phone call from Ann who had attended a corporate keynote speech I had delivered a few days earlier. She rang to tell me that she was going to 'send' her brother to me so I could 'sort him out'! So I told Ann that this isn't how it works. I said that he has to make the appointment, turn up on time, honour and commit to the process, pay the money and do whatever we agree is the 'homework'. I said that until he is ready for this she is well intentioned but wasting her time. She said, 'fine, but if you get a call from a Jimmy Blah Blah, you'll know who he is'. I assured her that I would as the surname she mentioned was an unusual one.

As you can probably imagine, in most of these cases the phone call never arrives, but in this case it did. At least someone left a totally messed up message but managed to blurt out his name before the time was up. Due to the surname I knew this was Jimmy and I phoned him back. We then had a really awkward phone conversation; he seemed really uncomfortable and nervous about the whole thing. So I decided to make him a special offer. I said that he seemed uncomfortable about all this so the special offer was, why don't we meet once (normally the initial commitment is three meetings) and if we ever met again it was up to him but he should at least experience one coaching session. He appreciated this offer and said yes, let's do it. When we looked at our diaries we realised that we were both near a particular city centre hotel that's good for meetings on the day that suited (if clients can't make it to my office I meet like this sometimes). So the meeting was arranged.

Meeting # 1

I arrived at the hotel lobby in good time. He was happy to meet in this hotel lobby as it's very large and although it is open plan it is divided up into quite private little areas. So I set up base camp and waited for Jimmy. He arrived on time looking very nervous and walked towards me without making any eye contact. I saw how nervous he was and decided that when he gets to me I'll say something funny to 'break the ice'. When he finally arrived I stood up, held my hand out to shake his and I said, 'welcome to my of-fice'. As he shook my hand he said:

'It's no wonder you f**king charge what you do if this is your office!'

I liked him immediately. I talked about coaching and what he could expect, I talked about how it all works and I mentioned that initially we'll need some objectives, some agenda – in other words, why is he here? He mentioned that he is 40+ years of age, runs a successful business in Dublin, it's going very well but his num-ber two guy is giving him a lot of trouble at the moment, but he said that today is about Jimmy, he doesn't want to talk about any-one else. He went on to say that he is separated from his wife, as amicable as it could be, can see his teenage children whenever he wants to, but he's lonely. He goes home to a big cold empty house every evening and he wants someone special in his life again. He went on to describe what the dream life for him would be (The Dream). I thanked him for his honesty and openness and we had a brilliant discussion around this.

At the end of the session I said, 'Right Jimmy, times up, thanks for coming, thanks for being so honest and open and sharing your life with me when it was uncomfortable to do so. I know what you want from this but please allow me to suggest where we start.'

(Note: I do quite a lot of work in this area and my usual ap-proach is to go back to Flying Lesson # 5 – The Value of Self-Worth, and you'll remember that people with high self-worth at-tract other people with high self-worth and then the relationship becomes a high worth relationship. Now, I've just met Jimmy, we had a great meeting, I don't have time right now to get into this, I'll explain to him another day. But he does need a little bit of discipline to get him moving again).

I then reminded him that during our meeting he had said that he used to go for walks in the evening time, found it to be a great help with many things but he'd fallen out of the habit of it. 'Jimmy,' I said, 'our starting point is three walks per week for four weeks; a minimum of 12 walks this month, that's your homework from today.

'Fair enough,' he said, 'that's fine with me.'

And then I restated what I said on the phone which was if he ever wants to meet again he knows where to find me.

Meeting # 2

A month later I'm waiting in the same hotel lobby. Jimmy arrives looking more upbeat this time. He waves and smiles as he walks towards me. He sits down, a bit further back in the couch this time, and seems in great form which I say to him. He replies that he is in great form and reports on his homework. First week about two walks, second week about five walks, third and fourth weeks he's walking every day, some days twice!

'I'm feelin' great, I've lost some weight, this is great, what's next?'

So we discussed time with his children, golf, and then we discussed his relationship with his 'number two guy' in work and why that wasn't working so well. When the session was over, I suggested to Jimmy that because he was feeling so good about himself that perhaps we could look for a stretch with his homework. We agreed the following:

✦ A minimum of three walks per week to continue

✦ One game of golf per week (as he had neglected this lately)

✦ And to talk to his 'number two guy' immediately to clear the air and get both of them back to performing better.

I ended the meeting by reminding him of our agreement which was if we ever meet again he knows where to find me.

Meeting # 3

A month later I'm ready in the hotel lobby area as usual. Jimmy is due any moment. He arrives on time but this time he walks into the lobby of the hotel like Frank Sinatra; he actually looks like he owns the place!

He's chatting up all the hotel staff, he glides across the lobby to where a guy is playing the piano and he has a bit of fun with him. Eventually he joins me and lies on the couch, feet and all. I now have Jon Bon Jovi in front of me!

'Well you've obviously got news?'

'Yep, but homework first . . .'

And he delivers the following report: still walking every day and it's super, played three games of golf badly but enjoyed them, and had-the-talk with the guy in work and everything is much better now, in fact, better than ever. But, that's not all …

Two weeks ago he was in the city centre, had just finished a meeting that went very well so he decided to reward himself (good for self-worth – 'lock-in' a victory with a reward). He said to me that this is **something he wouldn't normally do**. He went into a department store that he **wouldn't normally go into** and decided to buy himself some aftershave; he'd run out of it years ago. He went to the counter of the first brand he knew. The assistant was very helpful, perhaps a little too helpful because Jimmy couldn't decide between two types. At this point he noticed a female customer standing beside him – and he prefaced this again by saying to me,

'Neil, this is **something I wouldn't normally do**' – and he asked the woman which one of the two she prefers. She entered into the spirit of the moment and picked one. Jimmy said that that was the one for him and handed it to the assistant. While the assistant was processing the purchase Jimmy then 'did something, Neil, that I **wouldn't normally do**' and he turned to the woman and said:

'I don't want to make you feel uncomfortable or any-thing but you seem like a lovely person, would you meet me for a drink sometime?'

She thought about it for what seemed like an eternity and then said:

'No . . . but, I'll meet you for lunch!'

Bingo! There and then they exchanged first names, mobile phone numbers and agreed a lunch date for the following week.

The Lunch Date

Jimmy arrived early at the restaurant and made sure that he got the best table. He was looking fantastic and of course covered in aftershave! He texted Barbara to say he was there, where he was sitting and that there was no rush. Barabara arrived on time and when she arrived told the maître d' that she was meeting Jimmy who was already seated. The maître d' said, 'Of course, Mr. Blah Blah is here, please follow me'. Barbara hears Jimmy's surname for the first time and a tiny little connection happens deep in the back of her memory.

Barbara arrives at the table. Jimmy is overjoyed, tells her she looks fabulous, tells her he looks fabulous! Hopes she likes the aftershave? Barbara makes herself comfortable and as they are looking at the menu Barbara says to Jimmy:

'That's an unusual surname you have.'

Jimmy says:

'Yes, it's an old Dublin name. There are very few of us left.'

Barbara replies:

*'But I once knew a James Blah Blah from Walkinstown
in Dublin.'*

'Yes, James Blah Blah, Jimmy Blah Blah. That's me!'

In the next few moments they realise that they once knew each other. In fact, they were madly in love with each other when they were both 16 years of age! But then Jimmy's father told him to concentrate on his studies, stop playing sport and that he shouldn't have a girlfriend either. Based on this 'advice' Jimmy stopped seeing Barbara then and she was heartbroken. Thirty years later they met again at the aftershave counter.

This is of course a totally true story though I have changed both their names to protect their privacy. I'm still in touch with them, they are still in love and are also in business together. Turns out Barbara is as good a business person as Jimmy is.

Jimmy's Legacy

So what's the moral of the story? I believe there are a number of lessons from this and I hope that these also help to summarise the main messages in the book. Firstly, Jimmy was 'constructively discontent' with life and had a 'dream life' envisaged for himself. Then, although it was uncomfortable for him to do, he asked for help. He then set about through our coaching work to get some discipline and shape back into his daily routine. When he was feeling good about himself and acted on this he rewarded himself to 'lock-in' the feeling. He then was prepared to leave his comfort zone and do things 'he wouldn't normally do'.

Today Jimmy and Barbara and I are working on a new set of things that they wouldn't normally do, but are still worth doing.

And ultimately, Jimmy's current level of happiness, success and well-being can all be traced back to one starting point:

✦ Three walks per week

This is Jimmy's legacy: don't underestimate the power of injecting some discipline, some shape, some structure into your daily routine starting today. Remember, like walking, it has to be something that's good for you, that's easy to do and, most importantly, doesn't cost any money.

The Eagle and the Hen

I'd like to end by telling you the background to the name of this book and that also allows me to tell one of my favourite fables. I first saw it in a book by Anthony DiMello called *Awareness* and the following is my version of this story:

Once upon a time there was a young farmer who climbed mountains on his day off work. So one day he again got his climbing gear together, bid goodbye to his loved one and set off on his climb. It was a beautiful day for climbing and he was having a great time. Towards the end of his climb he had to negotiate a difficult ridge with a rocky outcrop. He was really challenged by this but made it on to the ledge. There he discovered an eagle's nest containing two eagle eggs.

Believing it to be a delicacy he took one egg, wrapped it very carefully in his towel and made his way home. At home he showed his find to his wife and she did not really want to cook and eat an eagle's egg – it just didn't seem right.

She suggested that they put the egg in the hen house, hatch it, and see what happens. So they did and 21 days later an eagle was born to the hens. It grew and lived as a hen.

Then one day in the farm yard the young eagle happened to be looking skyward, as it often did, and it saw a huge bird gliding effortlessly high above. It called it's mother over and asked what's that? The mother replied:

'Ah yes son, that's an eagle. The most powerful bird in the animal kingdom, magnificent isn't it? You see son, the eagle was born to fly and we were born to stay on the ground.'

During my last year in the bank I designed and delivered a personal development-type talk to various groups of the bank staff. I'd always finish this talk with the fable of the Eagle and the Hen and I would add my own 'punchline' so to speak:

'The eagle was born to fly and we were born to stay on the ground. But maybe you are an eagle and not the hen that you think you are. Maybe you should take a step because it could be … Your Time to Fly!

My talk became known as the Time to Fly Talk. Months later when I did leave the bank my accountant asked me, as we were setting up my business, what will we call it? I told him that that's easy, it's going to be called Time to Fly Ltd. He said that he liked the name but it'll probably be gone so I better give him another one. I said that it won't be 'gone' because it is waiting for me! He phoned me back an hour later to say congratulations, you are now the founder and owner of Time to Fly Ltd.

It's worth saying again: examine your programming, your conditioning, your self-perception – because you could be an eagle after all. The only way to find out is to do something you wouldn't normally do!

It's Your Time to Fly!

I look forward to meeting you on that rocky ledge!

PERSONAL NOTES AND ACTION PLAN

_____

_____

_____

_____

_____

_____

_____

_____

_____

_____

_____

_____

_____

_____

_____

_____

_____

_____

_____

Further Information

Neil O'Brien is an inspirational speaker, facilitator, coach and mentor. He travels the world speaking and coaching leaders in business and sport on his specialist topic of Mental Fitness.

Mental Fitness is the ability to become confident and motivated quickly, to stay this way longer than usual, and to be mentally tough and resilient in the face of constant change and challenge.

Neil also gives public talks and workshops through his company Time To Fly!

If you would like more information about Neil and his work he can be contacted at:

Time To Fly Ltd
78 Kincora Road
Clontarf, Dublin 3, Ireland
Phone: 003531 8339881
Website: www.timetofly.ie
Email: neil@timetofly.ie
Linkedin: Neil O'Brien
Twitter: @neilobriencoach
Facebook: Neil O'Brien